D1357917

Creed and Drama

AN ESSAY IN RELIGIOUS DRAMA

Creed and Drama

1368

W. MOELWYN MERCHANT

Professor of English, University of Exeter

FORTRESS PRESS · PHILADELPHIA

Published in Great Britain in 1965
by the Society for Promoting Christian
Knowledge, London

First published in the United States
in 1966 by Fortress Press, Philadelphia

FOR LYNNE
CHRISTINA AND
PAUL

Contents

Acknowledgements

I am profoundly grateful for the many opportunities over the years of discussing these problems with Mr Christopher Fry, whose own writings have so consistently illuminated them.

My gratitude is also due to my son Paul for the translations from Sophocles in the opening chapter.

Thanks are due to the following for permission to quote from copyright sources:

Actac (Theatrical and Cinematic) Ltd, *Thor with Angels*, by Christopher Fry,

The Editor, *Anglican Theological Review*, an article entitled "The Tragic Vision and the Christian Faith", by Nathan Scott.

Faber and Faber Ltd and Harcourt, Brace and World Inc., "Sweeney Agonistes" from *Collected Poems*; "Burnt Norton" from *Four Quartets*; *The Family Reunion*, by T. S. Eliot.

Faber and Faber Ltd and Farrar, Straus and Giroux Inc., "Poetry and Drama" from *On Poetry and Poets*, by T. S. Eliot.

Houghton Mifflin Company, *Chief Pre-Shakespearean Drama*, by J. Q. Adams.

Oxford University Press, *The Lady's Not for Burning, Curtmantle, The Dark is Light Enough*, by Christopher Fry.

Introduction

The shape, tone, and approach of this little book have been conditioned by its background and its present purpose. During 1957 the Religious Drama Society of Great Britain invited me to prepare a series of study outlines, one play for each month chosen from Sophocles to the present day. It was my aim in that series to recapture the serious tradition of the theatre and to correct some of the dangers which I felt to beset the practice of "Christian Drama". To reassess the credal content of *Antigone*, *Everyman*, *Lear*, Byron's *Cain*, Tennyson's *Becket*, Fry's *The Dark is Light Enough*, or Beckett's *Godot*, seems to me to open the possibility of questioning some of our present false didacticism and perhaps to halt the progress of religious drama in our day towards an amateurish and inbred cult. It seemed to me also to be an occasion for questioning our basic assumptions about the relation of creeds and liturgies to an art form, in this case the drama, and also to question our assumption about the Church and the theatre as instruments for the performance of our liturgies and our plays.

When, in the summer of 1963, Professor Massey Shepherd of the Divinity School of the Pacific, California, and Dean Alexander of the University of the South, Sewanee, Tennessee, invited me to lecture at the Sewanee Graduate School of Theology, I was given the opportunity of exploring these texts once more, in the presence of theologians and liturgists, and with research students who were themselves concerned with both the history and the presentation of liturgical drama. The gracious campus of Sewanee with its number of related disciplines in the arts and theology was a unique setting in which to test these assumptions. It should not be necessary to say that our presuppositions concerning religious drama require constant testing, by patient reading of drama from the past and by a vital sense of liturgy and of the significance of living theatre in our own day.

It would be an arrogant absurdity to attempt within the compass of a brief essay to write a "history of religious drama"; this little book makes no attempt even to be a popularization of scholarship. Rather it tries to trace one argument only, the relation between certain beliefs concerning human destiny and the dramatic form in which they were successively cast. It is not its aim to do justice to any period of dramatic history; Aeschylus and Euripides are not mentioned; nor is the Coventry cycle of plays; nor most of Shakespeare's contemporaries; few dramatists of to-day, even of those who have most significantly explored man's tragic nature, have been treated even briefly. I have chosen rather to allow one play to stand for an age and to choose those which were not only fine in their kind but representative of the speculations of their day and of its peculiar dramatic forms.

The phrase "religious drama" begs a number of questions and raises many others, some of them exceedingly teasing. It is quite clear that of some works of art we may properly expect affirmations, perhaps even some which could be called credal affirmations. But the degree of clarity with which the affirmation comes through will vary greatly. Our attention to belief in any concrete sense will be manifestly very different when we are considering Dante or Giotto, Brecht or Eliot, and in each of these cases they will be of a different order from similar considerations in Samuel Beckett or Camus. Moreover it should not need saying—though much writing about religious drama demands this caveat—that rarely can an affirmation be abstracted in a systematic way without impairing the integrity of any art form. The degree of intellectual affirmation will be greater in the *Divine Comedy* than in a fresco by Giotto, perhaps precisely to the extent that words make conceptual statements more readily than colour. But the *Divine Comedy* is done scant justice if we regard it as merely in some sort an imaginative translation of the *Summa*. It would be naïve to deny the Christian undertones of T. S. Eliot's plays; at the same time it would be uncritical to fail to see that Eliot's affirmations in the theatre must, in the nature of our culture, be more oblique than those of the Wakefield Master who wrote *Secunda Pastorum*.

This is not to say that art loses its integrity in all circumstances by assuming a didactic tone. *Everyman* is an effective sermon in the tradition of the medieval *exemplum*; Marlowe shakes an admonitory finger at the opening of the final chorus of *Faustus*:

> Cut is the branch that might have grown full straight
> And burnèd is Apollo's laurel bough,
> That sometimes grew within this learned man.
> Faustus is gone; regard his hellish fall.

One of the many complex undertones of "Guernica" comes from Picasso's passionate protest, its strong moral gesture; *The Crucible* derives much of its force—as well as some of its crudity —from Arthur Miller's involvement with the cultural and social predicament of the years in which it was written and the determined affirmations which it traverses. In none of these cases covering three centuries does didactic statement impair the integrity of the artist's work.

Nevertheless, we do well to respect the personal reticences of an artist. John Donne claims no such reticence; writing in the tradition of the "poetry of meditation", a form of poetic composition which involved the total exploration of a spiritual attitude or experience, he can pun in witty, devout, and scholarly fashion in a sermon at the very threshold of his own death. Preaching on "Death's Duell" at St Paul's, he closes with one of his greatest perorations:

> There wee leave you in that *blessed dependency*, to *hang* upon *him* that *hangs* upon the *Crosse*, there *bath* in his *teares*, there *suck* at his *woundes*, and *lie downe in peace* in his *grave*, till hee *vouchsafe* you a *resurrection*, and an *ascension* into that *Kingdome*, which hee *hath purchas'd for you*, with the *inestimable price* of his *incorruptible blood*. Amen.

The pun, "*dependency—hang*", wittily introduces the sonorous and moving conclusion on man's death in relation to the Crucifixion and Resurrection. Even more strikingly and again (though this time mistakenly) assuming death to be imminent, he wrote a meditative poem on the pressure of his sins, with a prayer for forgiveness. The refrain in the first two stanzas again displays wit as an instrument of gravity:

> When thou hast done thou hast not done
> For I have more

where the pun on "done" meaning both "finished with" and "completed" plays also on the poet's name. This security of spiritual tone, whereby wit becomes a valid tool of the poet's craft, implies a public articulation of attitude that is by no means universal in the other arts in the same age. Shakespeare was a contemporary of Donne; he explores profoundly an even wider range of matters which may properly be called religious; yet he makes no such personal declaration of his own credal position as Donne is enabled to produce in his lyric poetry. He is capable with dramatic integrity of establishing a Neo-platonic position, of creating a Machiavellian character, of informing a whole play with the traditional Christian assumptions on the forms of law (*Measure for Measure* is the most explicit, from its title onwards, as we shall see later); yet a collation of the passages where he quotes the Bible and the Book of Common Prayer would appear to argue one kind of personal orthodoxy in his work, while there have been equally powerful arguments for his being a Recusant writer. The critical decencies on our part demand that we should approach his work, like that of other artists of stature, prepared to accept the structure, the thought and image patterns, the movement of verse and character, to any point of interpretation which lies within the intellectual possibilities open in his day. This critical rule, a respect for either the reticence or the articulateness of the artist, carries with it the possibility of a valuable creative relationship between the artist and the theologian in the worship of the Church. For the thinker and the worshipper who are committed to the orthodox tradition there are necessary limitations to the "freedom of prophesying"; when speculation in creed or morals has reached a point where one further step would reach the border of heresy, and would make a creed invalid for the artist's recitation or make his reception of the sacraments deeply ambiguous, the artist would probably feel that he had to leave the Church. At the same time and on the other hand, if the Church itself is to remain creatively alive, speculation must be pushed to these limits of orthodoxy, and it is at this point that the exploration of the artist can be most vitally significant. Within the borders of his work his speculations are wholly free; their range, their complexity, their implications when pushed to the utmost of imaginative development, provide for the orthodox believer an area of creative relationship without which his beliefs might well become sterile or legalistic. We find these cultural growing points, exploring the images of belief, in all the arts of our own day; the necessarily limited studies which follow pursue, inside the patterns of our drama, some areas in which speculation has been far ranging. Indeed it may be suggested that the Pauline phrase, "the glorious liberty of the children of God", can be preserved in its richness only when the Church maintains an active relationship with writers and artists whose own liberty teeters on the very brink of heresy. It is a measure of the secure maturity of our theology and worship that we can, with equal courtesy and respectful attention, listen to Ferlinghetti and Camus, to Henry Miller and D. H. Lawrence, to Pinter and Albee; observe the extensive analyses of Picasso, the abstractions of Jackson Pollock and his successors, and desire that they revivify our fabric, our glass, and our vestments at the altar; listen to the creative tradition of Stravinsky and Alban Berg and hear it at last modify our own liturgical music.

I hope then that this book may be read—as it was substantially delivered in lecture form at the Sewanee Graduate School —as a brief text-book of experimental theology, a tentative handbook for those who wish to explore possible extensions of their liturgy and of their Christian insights in the field of the secular arts.

1

Classical Greece

It was a sound dramatic instinct which caused the medieval mind to extend Christ's descent on Easter Eve into a full symbolism of the Harrowing of Hell. For pre-Christian figures have to be brought into the orbit of the new dispensation, Abraham with Socrates, Moses with Plato, set down in the company of saints and martyrs. The same temper made Virgil a suitable guide for Dante to the very threshold of the beatific vision, while at more abstract levels to theologians of the Middle Ages Aristotle was supremely "the Philosopher".

Nevertheless, we must show some prudence in our expectations from the classical tragedian. What insights can the Christian who looks to drama as an imaginative expression of his faith expect from a pre-Christian dramatist? We have no hesitation in annexing the pre-Christian *Job* into the range of our insights; we understand when *Lear* distances the problems of value, rule, and human relationships into a natural order in a play which appears to set its age in a deliberately pagan context without the sophistication of theological statement; from the perspective of Christian theology the dramatic span from *Oedipus Rex* to *Antigone* can have an analogous relevance, a comment on the human condition without a route map of revealed theology to assist—or distort—our reading.

We do well from this viewpoint not to involve ourselves with too many considerations of the religious rites and beliefs out of

which sophisticated Athenian drama sprang. The study of
primitive Greek religion may be interesting and revealing to
the comparatist; it says little in the context of our present
limited inquiry. It is clear that the examination of character
and the sweep of event of which the Sophoclean trilogy consists
was in fact set within a highly developed religious celebration,
the spring festival of Dionysus at Athens, that though its
source and much of its temper eludes us, it manifestly em-
braced civic, artistic, even competitive elements within its religious framework. Moreover, though we are fortunate in the
quantity of drama that survives, a very much greater quantity
has disappeared, so that our knowledge of Athenian tragedy
depends upon our interpretation of the great dramatists of the
fifth century B.C., Aeschylus, Sophocles, and Euripides, and the
later rationalization of their practice in Aristotle's *Poetics*. With
one characteristic of their tragic material we are made very
familiar by the similar technique of Shakespeare's Histories.
Ismene's words to Antigone indicate that far more than an individual tragedy broods over the opening of the play; that
Ismene is involved in the same crisis as Antigone but it far
transcends them both.

> O, but think, my sister, how our father died—
> Hated and despised, when he himself
> With his own hands had struck at his own two eyes,
> Shamed by the sins his search laid bare.
> And then his wife, or mother—what you will—
> Took her own life in a noose of cords.

Sophocles proceeds to explore with the utmost ironic penetra-
tion the character of the central figure, revealing within the
tragic dignity with which she faces her dilemma both her stub-
born self-will and even her flashes of petulance. But the play is
more than a tragedy of character: it involves the long history of
a "dynasty", the family of Oedipus. This literary and historical
context is important. For if we read *Antigone* in its chronological

position as the third play in the trilogy after *Oedipus Rex* and *Oedipus at Colonus*, the words of Ismene appear naturally to refer back to earlier plays: "Do you forget how . . . ?" But though this play closes the tragedy of the Oedipus cycle, it was in fact the first play in that cycle to be written by Sophocles. This involves an important aspect of the Greek sense of time and of destiny in tragic drama. It has been assumed, with a great deal of justice, that a major difference between Greek tragedy (and its successors in Milton, the Restoration, and the French Classical Theatre) and Shakespearean, is that the latter involves the gradual unfolding of an act and its consequences, until the judgement implicit in the action is revealed in the course of time; while the former, the classical view of tragedy, involves the focusing of an issue and its complexity in one tragic crisis, succinctly presented. *Macbeth* and *Antigone* would seem to bear out this contrast. The former requires some months of implied action and a span from the corrupted court of Scotland to the benign English rule of the "pious Edward" to unfold the consequences of Macbeth's act in killing a king; on the other hand *Antigone* involves scarcely any such "working out" in time. The ingredients of the subsequent tragedy are totally present in the first few pages and the crisis is unfolded with terse inevitability; but this is a deceptive contrast. *Antigone*, though the earliest play in the group to be written, implies an actual knowledge shared by Sophocles and other members of his audience of the whole tragic story of the house of Oedipus. A just parallel would be the mental equipment and attitude of an audience at the first performance of the second part of *King Henry the Fourth*. Whether or not they had seen the first part, the dramatic tensions in the relation of Henry Bolingbroke to his son, the nagging unease of a throne wrested from the hand of Richard, the complex desire to turn a *de facto* ruling house into a *de jure* dynasty confirmed by the worthiness of the heir, account for the dark brooding of the whole of this play and the anticipation of the heroic kingship of King Henry V, transmuted from the scapegrace Hal. The tragic potentiality in this dynastic story exactly parallels the sense in Greek tragedy of momentous dynastic actions extended widely through time but focusing critically within the bounds of a single play, with the whole source material a common heritage of the dramatist and his audience.

Of greater importance then, as our background to a close critical reading of one or two of the plays of Sophocles, than any contrast we may sense in the structural methods of the Greek and English dramatists, is our understanding of what may in general terms be called the Greek dramatist's tragic view, and in particular of his recurring attempt to solve the problem, which Christian theology has described in terms of predestination and free-will, of the relation between the destiny of the individual, acting with his own personal integrity, and the foreknowledge of an omnipotent God who created him, or of an impersonal fate which broods over actions. This theme recurs in Aeschylus and Sophocles, and with laconic undertones in Euripides; it constitutes the intellectual background to the characteristic "Sophoclean irony" and is present in particular in both *Oedipus* and *Antigone*.

In general this problem recurs in three related moods. First, there is a continuing sense that tragedy is the outcome of the struggle of the human soul with a relentless "fate". This may be made concrete in prophecy such as the prophecy revealed to Laius and Jocasta at the birth of Oedipus, that he would murder his father and marry his mother. In this form the most terrible of the tragic ironies consists in the attempt to circumvent the prophecy's fate. In the logic of things the end is inevitable and the tragic poignancy is most fully revealed when the measures taken to avoid the inevitable themselves hasten its very consummation. This intuition of a predestined fate may also be seen in an active view of time as an agent, a revealing power which draws out the implications of the prophecy. In this mode it is closely analogous to the reliance upon a providential time in some of Shakespeare's comedies. When Viola is faced with the intolerable dilemma of loving a man who sends her as an emissary to the woman he loves, to be loved mistakenly in her turn by this woman, she withdraws into a relaxed trust in the inevitable:

> Time thou must untangle this not I,
> It is too hard a knot for me t'untie.

A second, contrasting mode of the tragic action focuses upon the outstanding responsibility of the individual, in that his tragic downfall is due to his own sin engendered by pride. To return to the Oedipus story: there is irony not only in the attempt by Laius and Jocasta to circumvent the prophecy; their assumption that they may succeed by their device of exposing the child to its fate is an arrogant reliance on human power in face of the inexorable. Within our own drama, the tradition of this mode of *hubris* gives tragic emotional depth to the rejection of the Delphic prophecy by Leontes, a prophecy which would have obviated the tragic alienations in the third act of *The Winter's Tale*.

A third and more creative mode of the tragic intuition is the sense that it issues in a final assertion of a divine order within the universe to which man must conform, even at the cost of seeing his self-will purged by pain and death. As we shall see, this is the assertion which produced the mysterious nobility in the closing movement of *Oedipus at Colonus*. We are similarly moved by the reassertion of due order by Malcolm in the last lines of *Macbeth*, by the humble reconcilation of Lear and Cordelia, even when the play takes a still further catastrophic plunge into agony, and by the submission of Job in face of an apparently incomprehensible fate. It is no accident that the Hebrew, Greek, and Christian world-picture shared a common assumption of Natural Law, of a universe whose basis is a lucid justice ultimately revealed despite the repeated invasion of lawlessness and catastrophe.

Oedipus Rex may at one level be studied as a growing investigation of irony until the final tragic moment when Oedipus insists upon the catastrophic revelation in the name of his own integrity. The ironies begin with an urbane, almost laconic tone in the conversation between Creon and Oedipus:

CREON
My Lord, before you governed us, we had
A King—his name was Laius—ruling us.

OEDIPUS
I knew him—only by hearsay; I never saw him.

This is spoken of his father whom he had seen with tragic consequences at "the place where three roads meet". The irony is intensified at the formal curse of him who should have been guilty of killing his father, concluding:

So I shall fight for him—just as I would
For my own father—yes, at any cost
I will find and take his murderer.

The entry of the prophet Teiresias not only thrusts forward the tragic complications, it recalls by his profession and cryptic speech the prophecy which preceded the play. His oblique condemnation of Oedipus is summarized in the dark aphorisms:

Just now he saw; not long ago
He owned a palace. Soon, a blinded wretch,
His stick shall lead him to a stranger's land.
As for the children of his house, he shall be found
Brother and father of them; mother's son
And husband; father's son and murderer.

The ironies are continued by the cynical attitudes of Creon to Oedipus:

CREON
Am I not equal to you and your Queen in Thebes?

OEDIPUS
Yes. Your friendship makes your crime more treacherous.

CREON
You would not say so by this reasoning—
Did you think that I would choose to rule
In constant fear, when I can live in peace,
And yet hold power?

But with this ironic moderation as a foil, the temper intensifies in the central scene between Oedipus and his wife/mother Jocasta. At the opening of the scene there is a buoyant and optimistic irony in the news which she predicts that his "father" Polybus is dead. But with his intensified wish to know the truth the tragedy knots into its final complexity. In a terrible pride, in total neglect of any compassion for Jocasta, Oedipus reverses the implication of the moral rule, *nosce te ipsum*:

JOCASTA
If you wish for life, in the name of God
Cease this search . . .

OEDIPUS
I cannot leave truth unexplored . . .
I desire no identity but my own by birth,
And must know who I am.

From this point the revelation becomes inevitable and the horror of incest forces him to a self-blinding which anticipates Gloucester's fate, with its agonized confession, "I stumbled when I saw".

The play would appear to have reached its tragic conclusion; but there are two further ironic impulses to thrust the play forward into the rest of the trilogy. Oedipus consigns the children to Creon ("Care for them, Creon"), those children who will be the core of the rebellious tragedy of *Antigone* and Creon's adversaries, while that tragedy is anticipated in ironic

detail through an oblique allusion to Creon's son, Haemon,
who was to be Antigone's lover: Oedipus laments:

> My blind eyes weep also for you, my daughters
> And prophesy a life of bitter misery—
> Many the time you will return in tears
> From parties scarcely begun, dinners untasted;
> And when your beauty ripens to the time of marriage
> Who will endanger himself with pollution then,
> Who bold enough to brave such foul contagion,
> Sharing with me and mine this weight of shame?

The proper conclusion of *Oedipus Rex* lies in the tragic serenity of *Oedipus at Colonus* and in particular in the messenger's
account of his mysterious translation in death, a removal from
life as mysterious as those of Moses and Elijah, types of our
Lord's Ascension:

> As for the way he died, no man can tell except Theseus. There
> was no thunderbolt of fire from God, no sudden whirlwind from
> the sea at that time. It was either some messenger from above or
> the earth opened to receive him below, in peace, not torment.
> For he died, this man, not in grief or disease or pain, but wonder-
> fully, not as mortals die.

Antigone, the first play of the trilogy to be written, and the
conclusion of the cycle, has made the greatest emotional impact on our sense of the tragic in our own day. Probably our
first impression is of starkly terse construction: within two
hundred lines of the play's opening, the "personal" problem
of Antigone has been declared (her agony at the contrast between the fates of Eteocles and Polynices), the Chorus has
hailed the victory of Thebes over the invader, and Creon has
established the laconic quality of his attitude:

> It is hard to gauge the true worth of a man,
> His temper, spirit and his mind, untried
> By the rigours of government and rule.

To this the Chorus gives its brief and ominous assent, in words which ironically summarize the tragedy to come:

> For those below and for us, still alive,
> Your word, my Lord, is law; we must obey.

The interlude of the Sentry follows, in a tone of wry comedy presenting the tragic disobedience of Antigone to Creon's edict (Shakespeare employs a similar ironic comedy at the highest moments of tragedy, not as "comic relief" but as interior, very complex comment on the tragic event: the drunken Porter, Lear's Fool, Enobarbus). The crisis both of character and argument is reached in Antigone's declaration to Creon:

> It was not God who issued that command,
> Nor did Justice make those laws for us,
> Who dwells with the gods below. You are only a man;
> I could not believe that your commands
> Could override by their own power the laws,
> Unwritten and forever sure, of God;
> Which live, not for to-day or yesterday, but evermore,
> While none may know their source.

(This passage expands the single majestic phrase in her early speech, "convicted of reverence".) The conflict now seems irreconcilable: Antigone stands for one aspect of universal, divine law, focused here in piety to her dead brother; but Creon also stands for a valid principle, the temporal order of the State; Sophocles appears, moreover, to redress our sympathies in the intellectual conflict by showing a darker, more triflingly arrogant side of Antigone, in her rejection of Ismene's loyalty:

> You may not die with me
> And what you dared not do
> Call not your own.

A new dimension is introduced with the entry of Haemon, Creon's son. To his love for Antigone is added a pungent assessment of his father Creon:

CREON
But have we not found her guilty?

HAEMON
All the people of Thebes think differently.

CREON
And will the city tell me how I ought to rule?

HAEMON
Do you not see how childish that is?

CREON
Am I not king? or will some other rule the State?

HAEMON
And can you call a single man a State?

CREON
Is not a city governed by its king?

HAEMON
I think that you would rule a desert well.

The king's wilful sin is to work itself out still further, until, with the death of his son and of his wife, Eurydice, his will is broken.

> My hands hold only wickedness
> And of my hope I bear
> A legacy of grief unbearable.

The implications of this tragic conflict have been implicit throughout the play's action: the imperious will of Creon, corrupting itself even while attempting the moral good of an ordered State, and the tragic inheritance of Oedipus, working itself out in the equally imperious piety of Antigone. The frontiers between statecraft, moral choice, and religious promptings are not rigidly marked—as they never can be, in life or art.

The theme is pursued in our own day; Anouilh is an uncomfortable, astringent writer, capable of a twisted ironic grin at man's naïveties, but never denying the nobility of man, even when, as in *Antigone*, he rejects "le sale espoir" as an invalid dream. (The dignity within the caustic rejection of flimsy pieties in the modern French theatre cannot be ignored. Sartre, Giraudoux, Anouilh, confront our easy assumptions with a proper seriousness.)

Produced in 1944, *Antigone* has been described (somewhat inadequately) as "a rallying statement of the French Resistance against German tyranny". In fact Anouilh holds the balance between Creon and Antigone far more tenderly than Sophocles. There is real compassion for Creon, who "practises the difficult art of a leader of men"; there is still greater compassion for Antigone, who, at the end of the play, "is calm to-night and we shall never know the name of the fever that consumed her". Between these two compassions the play moves with a deep understanding of character (and without condemnation), with a view of tragedy as the final release, the freedom of the personality: "Antigone has been caught. For the first time in her life, little Antigone is going to be able to be herself".

This conception of tragedy, so different from Sophocles and so different from the Christian, requires our main attention. It is stated in abstract by the Chorus:

Tragedy is restful; and the reason is that hope, that foul, deceitful thing, has no part in it . . . In melodrama, you argue and struggle in the hope of escape . . . But in tragedy, where there is no temptation to try to escape, argument is gratuitous: it's kingly.

This apparent renunciation becomes active, militant, in Antigone. Though Creon, in a long and subtle argument, debases her picture of Polynices, even of human happiness itself, she destroys his argument with her outburst:

I spit on your happiness . . . We are of the tribe that asks questions and we ask them to the bitter end . . . We are of the tribe that hates your filthy hope . . . Father became beautiful. And do you know when? At the end. When all his questions had been answered. When he could no longer doubt that he *had* killed his own father; that he *had* gone to bed with his own mother . . When it was absolutely certain that nothing, nothing could save him. Then he was at peace; then he could smile, almost; then he became beautiful.

A tragedy with that affirmation at its core demands our respect and our attention.

2

Medieval Liturgical Drama

In the history of religious drama, medieval liturgical forms provide the crucial test for our discrimination; this is the point in the development of dramatic writing at which it is most important that the correct questions be asked, literary, theological, and liturgical. For in the group of texts now to be considered, the Passiontide and Nativity tropes, we have dramatic action and liturgical rite in the closest conjunction. This appears to be the perfect type of religious drama; moreover, its growth and elaboration, its increasingly complex relationship with the liturgy of the Church, extended over some four centuries, until increasing "secularization", a growing "theatricality", forced the drama out of the chancel into the market-place. Here then are the two central questions: What was the nature of the relationship between the dramatic act and the liturgy in which it was set? and, Why should it have become necessary to continue this dramatic development outside the walls of the church which had been its home for some centuries?

The indispensable source-book for this liturgical drama is the monumental study by Karl Young, *The Drama of the Mediaeval Church* (O.U.P., 2 vols., 1933). His method and approach best illustrate the fundamental dilemma confronting any student of this drama. He opens with an analysis of the Roman Mass and the Canonical Office, proceeds to examine "Dramatic and other Literary Aspects of the Roman Liturgy" and so to consider the dramatic texts themselves. Very properly he distinguishes worship (and especially the rite of the Eucharist, man's participation in divine reality) from drama, which is essentially imitative. It is useful at this point to sharpen the distinction verbally by opposing "reality" and "imitation" (*mimesis*) as the two categories which separate worship from drama. For there is an uneasy ambiguity throughout Karl Young's argument, which employs "impersonation" as the *differentia* of drama. It scarcely requires saying that the celebrant at the Eucharist, though he may be said "to imitate acts of Christ himself" yet "does not attempt impersonation, and hence he is not an actor at a play".

Yet, when Young comes to examine the part played by clerics in speaking (or singing) the words of the Marys, angels, shepherds, in the "dramatic interpolations" with which we are concerned, he finds it exceedingly difficult to decide the point at which impersonation has truly become the intention. He more readily admits the element of impersonation to be present when the dramatic actions take place within the Day Hours than when a similar action is interpolated in the Mass. A proper reverence for the more intense moment of worship has probably unconsciously blurred the purely literary judgement.

It is almost certainly safer to abandon this exclusive concern with the *persons* of the action and their theatric status, and to look at the total dramatic action, taking together its elaboration, intensity, and duration; its dependence upon and separation from the words of the liturgy; in sum, its final aim, which must ultimately be decided by the question: Is this dramatic interpolation a valid heightening and extension of the moment of worship, preserving a comely proportion within the liturgy, or has it grown beyond the ends of worship and become dramatic, mimetic in its own right?

The beginnings, in the tenth century, have clear characteris-

tics. The most important is the connection with the *music* of
the liturgy. Certain moments in the worship, notably the festal
Alleluias, had elaborate extensions of their musical settings
(the final *a* sometimes lengthened to cover a group of melodic
phrases); words were added to these melodies, together con-
stituting *proses* or *sequences*, and when they took on dramatic
shape they became known as *tropes*. One of the earliest of these,
the *Quem quaeritis* from a tenth-century manuscript at St Gall,
has a deceptive brevity and simplicity when it is written:

> Whom seek ye in the sepulchre, O followers of Christ?
> Jesus of Nazareth, who was crucified, O celestial ones.
> He is not here, he is risen as he foretold; go, declare that he is
> risen from the sepulchre,

but sung (not spoken) and accompanied by its brief procession,
it has already, in this germ of a play, a certain formal elaboration. By the time we reach the text from the *Winchester Troper*,
written in 979, comment through antiphonal melodies has considerably extended the form (there are two antiphons given to
the choir). The rubrics now take on the appearance of elaborate
"stage directions", implying a considerable degree of "impersonation", even though subordination to the proper end of
liturgy is wholly maintained:

> ... While the third responsory is being sung, let the remaining
> three follow, all of them vested with copes and carrying in their
> hands censers filled with incense and slowly, as though seeking
> something, let them come before the place of the sepulchre.
> These things are done in imitation of the angel seated in the
> tomb and of the women coming with spices to anoint the body
> of Jesus ...

The logical extension of this form is found in the thirteenth-
century trope from Orleans, in which three episodes have
crystallized out: Visits to the Sepulchre by the Marys, and by
Peter and John, and the Resurrection Appearance to St Mary

Magdalene. This closes with the very moving appearance of our
Lord to the women:

> ... Let him who has formerly been the Gardener come in the
> likeness of the Lord ...

and, splendidly vested, he declares that he will meet them in
Galilee. The choir responds,

> Alleluia! Resurrexit hodie Dominus

and continues with an act of adoration:

> Leo fortis, Christus, Filius Dei!

the whole dramatic structure ending with the Te Deum.

Meanwhile, other dramatic rites had developed, notably the
Burial and Resurrection of the Cross. We have our most fasci-
nating accounts from Durham; the first in a missal of the fourteenth century (doubtless reflecting earlier practice, for the
Depositio Crucis is known from the tenth century onwards and
there are numerous "Easter Sepulchres" in England); the
rubrics imply an action in three elaborate "movements": the
Cross is brought into the choir and the adoration is accompanied by an antiphon and responsory; the Cross is taken to the
Sepulchre, while five antiphons are sung; the procession returns
to the choir, the antiphon "Joseph ab Arimathia" is sung and
the celebrant vests for the Mass of the Presanctified. Before the
Suppression of the Monastaries we have a description in English
of the Depositio and Elevation at Durham:

> Within the Abbye Church of Durham, uppon Good Friday,
> theire was marvelous solemne service, in the which service time,
> after the Passion was sung, two of the eldest Monkes did take a
> goodly large Crucifix all of gold, of the picture of our Saviour
> Christ nailed uppon the crosse ... and all the Monkes after [the
> Prior] in the same order [adored the cross]; and in the mean time
> all the whole quire singing an himme. The service beinge ended,
> the two Monkes did carrye it to the Sepulchre with great

reverence, which Sepulchre was sett upp in the morninge on the north side of the Quire, nigh to the High Altar, before the service time; and there lay it within the said Supulchre with great devotion . . . settinge two tapers lighted before it, which tapers did burn unto Easter day in the morninge, that it was taken forth.

Here then, shorn of the many hundreds of variants recorded by Young, is the growth of a liturgical dramatic form, spanning many centuries of medieval worship, and subservient to the ends of that worship; in words and music these interpolations are wholly congruous with the movement and temper of the liturgy in which they find their origin and setting; the melodies are those of the plain-chant setting of the rite, the words are taken from the scriptures or they are antiphonal elaborations of the scriptures. The worshipper would have no sense other than that of a heightened dramatic intensity, as the rite pauses for its brief elaboration. Whether the tropes are interpolated into the Eucharist or the Offices (of Mattins or Vespers or any other of the Hours), the temper is the same, a humble subordination to the end of worship.

It seems clear that the origins and development of the Nativity tropes run parallel to those of the Passion or at least follow closely upon them. The initial forms of each may be seen in their original words:

> Quem quaeritis in sepulchro, O Christicolae?
> Quem quaeritis in praesepe, pastores, dicite?
>
> Jesum Nazarenum crucifixum.
> Salvatorem Christum Dominum.
>
> Ite, nuntiate quia surrexit.
> Nunc euntes dicite quia natus est.

From these beginnings the growth of the Nativity tropes was by elaboration of the scriptural incident with comment by antiphon, as we have seen in the Passion texts. By the thirteenth century there were finely wrought forms of the Pastores,

Magi, and Herodes tropes, which, whether plainly spoken or set to music, would very amply fulfil their former rôle in our churches. One of these plays, from a fourteenth-century text at Rouen, has a most attractive indication of a dramatic "prop":

> When the procession begins to enter the nave of the church, let the corona [a chandelier in the form of a crown] hanging before the cross be raised in the fashion of a star.

The Magi point to the "star" and chant the antiphon, "Ecce stella in Oriente".

Deriving in manner from both the Passion and Nativity tropes are the numerous independent plays on scriptural themes from both the Old and New Testaments and the many Saints' plays, notably those on St Mary Magdalene, the Conversion of St Paul, and the very popular St Nicholas plays. These flourish from the eleventh to the fourteenth centuries and clearly foreshadow the elaborately organized "cycles" of the Craft Guilds, with which we are not here concerned.

It probably needs far more patient effort to recreate the mood and intention of these early tropes than we require to understand almost any other aspect of religious drama. The complexity of the material deployed by Karl Young need not trouble the student who is content with the less exacting texts in the first eighty pages of J. Q. Adams' *Chief Pre-Shakespearean Dramas* (1924), from which I have deliberately taken all my examples here. What requires more historical imagination is the temper imposed on these texts by the fact that they were *sung*, incorporating traditional anthems, responses, and Psalms, and entirely *within* the liturgy, seeking no independent life apart from the daily rite of the Church. The gestures of "performances" would be those of the celebrant, as we know them to our own day, formal, utilitarian, rhetorical in the original sense, neither "naturalistic" nor "theatrical" as the theatre has known gesture and movement since the eighteenth cen-

:ury. The costumes were those of the sacred Ministers, with :heir complex significances; the colours the allusive, symbolic :olours of the liturgical year (though Cain in the *Mystère d'Adam* and St Mary Magdalene almost throughout these works wear red, a "realistic" and not a liturgical suggestion of character).

It would be rash, on the conflicting evidence, to suggest that the late medieval rejection of this drama by the ecclesiastical authorities was on any consistent moral or theological grounds. By the fourteenth century the interpolated tropes had grown to their greatest elaboration and length if they were properly to remain as adjuncts to a liturgical action, without over-weighting it. Once severed from the liturgy, the plays of the craft cycles were free to make comment, to extend their themes with a didacticism completely absent from the tropes, and with a theatricality which would have been offensively in-appropriate in them.

A humble consideration of the limits within which the creators of these tropes were prepared to work would seem to indicate the propriety (and impropriety) of the dramatic forms which we employ to-day in our churches. The medieval church was an instrument for worship and it was suitable only for such dramatic experiments as the expansion of the liturgy itself, by trope or mimed action. It was as unsuitable as most modern churches for seeing and hearing anything in the nature of "theatre", apart from the incongruity which it felt in engaging in such action.

To-day the situation has been made complex by our mixed architectural inheritance. Surviving Gothic churches, together with their counterparts of the Victorian Gothic revival, give us splendid instruments for the sounds of sung worship, even if they are generally quite inadequate for the preaching of ser-mons and *a fortiori* for the hearing of "liturgical drama", however that phrase be interpreted. At the same time the modern liturgical movement with its central stress on lay participation in the liturgy has quite radically shifted our feeling for the shape of our churches, the relation of altar to chancel and nave, giving a renewed sense, derived from the early Church, of "doing and seeing the liturgy"; indeed quite a startling parallel is revealed between the idea of participation in the liturgical act and the movement in the secular theatre towards involving the audience in the action by such architectural modification as the platform stage and "theatre in the round".

While there may be some unexamined assumptions in these two parallel ideas of "participation" and "involvement" which will soon demand exploration both by our liturgists and by theatre specialists in their several worlds, there can be no doubt that the climate is changing towards the necessity of our having such experiments as "chancel drama", already in train in Germany and the United States and, sporadically, in Great Britain. It is an important speculation also to determine whether we have now sufficient confidence in the vitality of our worship together with sufficient liturgical flexibility to attempt such dramatic extensions of our liturgy as the medieval Church found possible, seemly, and spiritually stimulating in its early tropes. In the Eucharist this would seem possible and appropriate at such moments as the Gradual; in the Divine Office at the Canticles, or, when the Office is over, in place of the sermon, when the season or the lessons make such an extension of the Church's active liturgy possible. It may well be that with moderation and due safeguards this is a necessary touchstone for the sincerity and proper vitality of our liturgical revival.

Writers and artists occasionally reveal themselves with the most startling clarity at apparently quiet moments in their work. The two *Shepherds' Plays* from the "Wakefield Cycle" have this feature in common. *Prima Pastorum* closes with the worship of the Child by the three shepherds; the second shepherd addresses him: "Haylle, lytyle tyne mop!... Hayle, David sede!" and the third shepherd employs the same apparent incongruity:

> Haylle, maker of man! haylle, swetyng!
> Haylle, so as I can, haylle, praty mytyng!

where the affectionate adoration moves from a recognition of the Creator to his incarnation in the "pretty mite". *Secunda Pastorum* ends with the same union of rapt affirmation with human affection:

> Hayll, comly and clene! hayll, yong child!
> Hayll, Maker as I meyne! of a madyn so mylde ...
> Lo, he laghys, my swetyng!...
>   Have a bob of cherys!

Such security in reverence, moving swiftly from adoring humility to an amused tenderness before the Child, is a quality we shall find throughout these two plays, and their similarity has led many scholars to suppose the single hand of a "Wakefield Master", either in writing or in revising these plays. (He is credited also with the *Cain and Abel* play.)

But this Master remains unidentified, in company with many other medieval masters—masons, illuminators, painters, sculptors, and musicians, and he raises, with them, the teasing question of "medieval anonymity". Some speak of it as though it were a humble virtue, a restraint from self-assertion, a recognition that the Body of Christ was greater than its individual limbs and members. But this is to exalt an accident into a principle. In so many instances, as in these two plays, the artistic personality stands revealed in everything but name. He is as vivid as the portrait of Master Jordan the carpenter in the thirteenth-century triforium at Westminster or the grave self-portrait of Peter Parler a little later in Prague cathedral. In the period which spans these craft plays, we know with no anonymity the work of Chaucer, Langland, Gower, and Lydgate, in letters; of Dunstable, Redford, and Taverner, in music; of Henry Yevele as master in a host of master-builders; and if carpenters, painters, and sculptors are figures a little less clear in outline, that is only because their crafts took a humbler place in the medieval scheme of things.

This "Wakefield Master" then, like many a "Master of the Monogram", is an individual, recognizable, technically anonymous, but in no way self-effacing. One of the pleasures of wrestling with a somewhat unfamiliar spelling and syntax is that with its mastery comes a recognition of a still-living drama written by a man whose accents and tones are distinguishable.

When the craft guilds took over from the clerisy the presentation of drama, the strictly liturgical phase in religious drama came to an end. During the whole of the fourteenth and the greater part of the fifteenth century, the guild cycles dominated popular drama, while the more sophisticated didacticism of the morality plays slowly emerged. The physical presentation of these plays, the "pageants" at the several "stations" in a city, is tolerably well known, and concentration on the stage machinery or property-lists has fostered the illusion of their "crudity" or, with even less happy condescension, their "charming naïvety". A closer examination of their theological intentions and their (perhaps unconscious) literary qualities, may correct these errors.

Four cycles of plays have survived and their most striking quality is their comprehensive sweep of event; based on the scriptures, they are literally cosmic in their theological range, embracing Creation, the Fall, human history, Incarnation, Redemption through the Cross, Resurrection, Ascension, and the "Last Things". The longest cycle we now possess, the York, takes forty-eight episodes or plays to compass this narrative (we have had the fortunate opportunity in recent years to see its form and magnitude in E. Martin Browne's presentation at

York). The Chester cycle is the shortest surviving group with twenty-five plays, the Townely (Wakefield) cycle has thirty-two and the Coventry forty-two. The action confines itself within the biblical incident and is of necessity limited and spare in technique. Where the action and dialogue is expanded, it is strictly congruous with the intention of the biblical narrative, amplifying its emotional significance or its dramatic (or occasionally theological) implications. Thus the pathos and submissiveness of Isaac are developed in the "non-cycle" Abraham play from the Brome manuscript beyond the clear directness of the Genesis story, while the "comedy" in the Cain and Shepherd plays in the Wakefield group, so far from being a decorative addition, belongs to the core of the author's interpretation of Cain and of the Incarnation.

We ought to reckon in our interpretation of the plays on the almost consistent attitude of the Church towards them. There were many traditional reasons for rejecting dramatic works altogether: the distinction, going back to classical Greece, between "fiction" and literal or philosophic truth and the abiding conflict between Appearance and Reality, between Mask and Person; the antipathy of the Church Fathers to the licentious and sadistic extremes of late Latin comedy; the growing medieval conviction that man's redemption was too grave a matter for the levity of dramatic delineation. A succession of enactments forbade clerics to take part in drama, and banned play-production in church, but the attitude is subtler than that implied in formal law; a recent scholar has expressed it as "the silence or mild contempt of earnest orthodox churchmen of the fourteenth or fifteenth century, who regarded the plays, as indeed many have done ever since, as 'drawing men to inanities' away from their devotions and the more solemn and pressing demands of God's word in the pulpit".

Yet in spite of this focusing of a long tradition of rejection, the guild cycles evolved a powerful dramatic statement and even

benefited from the "secularization" enforced on them; for the
action to take place outside the strictly liturgical setting enabled both writers and players to intensify the theatric qualities of their work and broaden the range of its interpretation.
The work of the "Wakefield Master" shows this process at its
height.

There is, however, a danger of falsification in isolating two or
three apparent masterpieces from the plays conceived as
cycles. Our experience in reading should be as near as possible
to that of a medieval spectator at a full day's "station" at a
complete cycle. An interesting alternative study is to follow the
biblical narrative of Creation—Redemption—Judgement in a
selection from all cycles, such as that of Adams in *Chief Pre-
Shakespearean Dramas*.

The existence of two "pastoral plays" in one cycle is itself
something of a puzzle. It is scarcely a just appraisal of them to
regard *Prima Pastorum* as a journeyman piece preparing for the
master-work of *Secunda Pastorum*; the former play has too
assured a grasp of dramatic structure for this rôle, it is too allusive in language, too complete in characterization to be appren-
tice work. Its structure within the briefest compass (some five
hundred lines) is this: the wintry misery of man in this mutable
world is declared by the three shepherds; the miraculous feast
is conjured up from apparently empty scrips; the angels' pro-
clamation of the Birth; the adoration and the gifts of the
shepherds.

The opening movements, the suffering of the poor and the
strange feasting, are conducted with some wry humour:

> I may syng
> With purs penneles
> That makes this hevynes!

but for all the apparent levity, the suffering is real enough.
With the end of the feast and the transition to the angels' song,

more serious significances are shown. The feast, amplitude in the midst of poverty, proves more than satisfying for the shepherds and they make to gather the fragments into "panyers", until the third shepherd exhorts them:

> For our saules let us do
> Poore men gyf it to.

In an age of faith, the eucharistic significances within this re-collection of the miraculous feeding of the multitude would not be lost. From this point to the end the scriptural move-ment is followed in dignified verse (with a witty excursion into Virgil by the third shepherd!) until the pattern of redemption in Christ closes the play.

> We mon alle be restorde, God grant it be so!

The Second Shepherds' Play opens with the same destitution:

> No wonder, as it standys, if we be poore,
> For the tylthe of our landys, lyys falow as the floore.

The three shepherds in this play are joined by Mak, thief, liar, and adept at dark arts. He steals a sheep from them and this is the occasion of the "mock-nativity" of the sheep in the cradle. This is no "farcical interlude" but is as complex and allusive as the feast in the former play: there are hints of the sheep "lost and found", anticipations of the true worship at the manger, and, over all, an indulgent charity and compassion shown even to the rogue—a temper extended into the final movement of the play, in the angel's affirmation:

> God is made your freynd now at this morne.

Neither play, then, is a pious nativity leavened by a comic in-terlude. Rather they are complementary in their serious ex-ploration of man's fallen nature (which can be gross, grotesque, pitiful, and pitifully comic, a matter for laughter and the source of it) taken up into the joy of redemption. If there is "freedom from the Church" here, it does not produce something alien, heterodox, daring—or more literary. The treatment of comedy as well as the reverent worship in these plays is equally orthodox and congruous with scripture; but it has burst the bounds of liturgy and moved outwards towards the theatre.

Readers of Owst's monumental volume, *Mediaeval Preaching*, will need no reminding of the powerful tradition of pulpit didacticism in the Middle Ages. From the brilliant parody of an *exemplum* in Chaucer's *Pardoner's Tale* to the full close of the medieval tradition in Wycliffe's *Sermon of the Plough*, the vitality of the preaching tradition makes the parallel theatrical growth of the Morality play inevitable. Fewer plays of interest and dramatic competence have survived from this form of medieval drama than from the tradition of the pure liturgical drama, but *Everyman* and the *Castle of Perseverance* have their own distinction, and last year at the Tower Theatre, Canonbury, London, Skelton's *Magnyfycence* was revived after four centuries. This play was a political and moral warning to the young Henry VIII against the overweening power of Wolsey. A dramatic critic of *The Times* found that this was no "neglected masterpiece. The homiletic sections are mostly as flat on the stage as they are in the text". But before considering briefly its more distinguished rivals in this genre, the quality of *Magnyfycence* should be noted. Superficially, it would be assumed to be a characteristic late medieval "war for the soul", a struggle between embodied virtues and vices, which reached its most brilliant sophistication in Marlowe's *Faustus*. Skelton, however, was not only an instructed medieval moralist; he was sufficiently a child of the Renaissance to take as his central figure the Aristotelian virtue of magnificence as the quality which especially graced the great man and the ruler. Spenser was to develop this to its conclusion in the text of Christian virtue in

The Faerie Queene. This wedding of Aristotelian and Christian categories gives Skelton the opportunity for an exercise in a central problem of moral discipline, the conflict between proper pride and humility, the exploration of that moment when *amour propre* becomes corrupted into the cardinal sin of pride.

This dramatic examination of moral problems is characteristic also of the greater Moralities, and the most critical problem is to determine the essential *dramatic* success with which the translation of moral terms has been made in the theatre. But we should be quite clear in our sympathetic understanding of the form and the qualities in which it differs from its predecessors in the liturgical tradition. There the tropes and their mature successors were offshoots of the liturgical *worship* of the Church; the morality is kin to the *preaching* office of the Church; it declares—and in this it is unashamedly didactic—a theological or moral truth. In a sense which does no serious violence to its intention, it is a dramatized sermon. Its shape is therefore argumentative and not necessarily dramatic in the theatrical sense; since virtue will be at war with vice, the protagonists will tend to be abstractions, bringing a great number of difficulties to the dramatist. Moreover there is the teasing ambiguity that Man is at once the battlefield over which the struggle takes place and at the same time the chief protagonist. He is at once the being whose eternal condition is the subject of the play and it is his warring elements, the virtues and vices of his disposition, which constitute the *dramatis personae.* The perfect type of this dramatic ambiguity may be found in *Everyman* (a simpler and more immediately comprehensible play than *The Castle of Perseverance*) in which Man together with his disparate elements, Good Deeds, Beauty, Strength, and so on, are on the stage at the same time; Man is conceived both as an organic unity, a "soul" moving towards an eternity of bliss or terror, and as an analysable bundle of separate parts, some co-operating, many of them struggling against each other. In pedantic hands this might produce a very dull sermon indeed; in *Everyman* and *Perseverance* it produces high art.

If this transformation of the sermon pattern into dramatic form is to take place, then there must be conflict, with the possibility that there may be a tragic conclusion. Fundamentally the conflict need not be (indeed, cannot be wholly) external, as Prudentius demonstrated a thousand years earlier than our present anonymous author, when he wrote his *Psychomachia* (*The War of the Soul*). But from the very conception of the stage setting itself, the conflict in *Perseverance* is externally dramatized. The "theatre" is conceived in three concentric circles, with the audience presumably surrounding the outermost. Within is the castle itself and around it runs a moat, so that the inner playing area is kept completely free for the characters who descend within the moated space. Outside the moat are five scaffolds, four at the points of the compass— God in the east, World in the west, the Devil in the north, and Flesh in the south. To the north-east is a scaffold for Covetyse. The action moves with the utmost flexibility between these five focal points, the open "plateau", and the central castle itself.

Within the bounds of this dramatic setting, with its emotive medieval reference to the protective keep of a Norman castle, the author sets his struggle for the welfare of Mankind's soul. And here a further literary association must be kept in mind, the tradition of the *Ars Moriendi*, the Art of Dying, or rather of so living that a "good death" is inevitable. These are moral treatises, of which the most famous later examples are Jeremy Taylor's *Holy Living and Holy Dying* and Bunyan's *Pilgrim's Progress*. These were dramatic for all their didacticism, in an age which truly believed in an eternal state and the palpable conflict of angelic hosts. *The Castle of Perseverance* itself ends significantly:

Thus endyth our gamys.
To save you fro synnynge,
Evyr at the begynnynge,
Thynke on your last endynge!
Te Deum, laudamus!

Though the dramatic setting of *The Castle of Perseverance* is
theatrically interesting and especially to us in its anticipation of
"theatre in the round", *Everyman* is clearly the Morality which
has best survived the centuries. It is firmly articulated in structure with some moving passages of rhetorical and emotional
writing. Its theme is familiar, for it is still fairly frequently
played. Death is the servant of God as his "myghty messen-
gere". To summon him to his final pilgrimage Everyman at
once reckons his human resources, and in two adjacent passages
a relation of wit and gravity effectively establishes a theatrical
convention.

EVERYMAN
My Cosyn, wyll you not with me go?

COUSIN
No, by Our Lady! I haue the crampe in my toe.
(*Everyman goes to his Riches for help*)

EVERYMAN
All my lyfe I haue had ioye and pleasure in the,
Therefore, I pray the, go with me.

RICHES
Naye, Everyman, I saye no.
As for a whyle I was lente the;
A season thou hast had me in prosperyte.
My condycyon is mannes soule to kylle;
Yf I saue one, a thousand I do spyll.

With this rejection he turns to Good Deeds and the Seven
Sacraments who lead him to the brink of the grave:

EVERYMAN
Into thy handes, Lorde, my soule I commende,
Receyve it, Lorde, that it be not lost.
(*Everyman and Good Deeds descend into the grave*)

ANGEL

Come, excellente electe spouse to Iesu!
Here aboue thou shalte go,
Because of thy synguler vertue.
Now the soule is taken the body fro,
Thy reckenynge is crystall clere.
Now shalte thou in to the heuenly spere;
Unto the whiche all ye shall come
That lyueth well before the daye of dome.

Thus endeth this morall playe of Eueryman.

This complex tradition of drama wholly dependent on the
Church's teaching and worship has an active life-span of five
hundred years. By the end of the sixteenth century the temper
had changed, and with Marlowe's *Faustus* a new age in dramatic
presentation of theological matters had begun.

3

Marlowe's *Doctor Faustus*

The publication of Marlowe's *Dr. Faustus* at the opening of the
seventeenth century marks an important watershed in the
development of religious drama. There is now no ambiguity
about the nature of the dramatic act. It is totally severed from
both the worship and the teaching of the Church and is firmly
a part of public theatre. This first considerable play handling
religious themes in the secular tradition is moreover the work
of one of the most enigmatic figures in English literature.
Christopher Marlowe, Parker Scholar from Canterbury to
Cambridge, whose career showed some indications of an intention to take Holy Orders, earned the reputation of "atheism"
in his lifetime and died young in a tavern brawl. Both *Tambur-
laine* and *Faustus* have been interpreted in widely different
senses and this chapter will concentrate on a very limited
aspect of the latter play.

Some figures in literature appear so firmly embedded in
fiction that it is scarcely possible to credit their existence in fact.
Such a figure is John Faust, who appears down the centuries
with almost incredible persistence, in drama, chap-books,
ballads, poems, and the puppet-plays which still amuse German children. The central character, Faust, has gathered to
himself magic, buffoonery, the profoundest philosophy, the
deepest devilry, and the most romantic love. It is almost un-
believable that there was at one time an original, living Faust;

the facts are that he lived from about 1488 until 1541, that he was born at Knittlingen, in the Rhine Palatinate, and that at the University of Heidelberg he was the most distinguished student of his year.

Yet even during his lifetime legends began to gather about this remarkable man. He was wild in his living, and ventured into so many by-ways of strange learning, that it was said that he received the aid of the devil. Finally, so the story went, he died a horrible death and the devil received his soul. One recent writer comments: "Faust, the scholar and friend of von Sickingen, Melanchthon, and Luther . . . has become Faust the tramp—tramp of that type common to all times, silver-tongued but depraved, fine-brained but ill-balanced, the European beachcomber of the sixteenth century."

Out of this strange material there grew the Faust literature which includes some of the finest writing in drama and poetry. The first to treat the theme seriously was Marlowe in *The Tragical History of Doctor Faustus*, written about 1589 and published in 1604. This is a study in a scholar's overwhelming desire for knowledge which will make him god-like and the damnation which overtakes him.

The text as we have it is very imperfect; there are certainly additions, mainly in the farcical elements in the play, by other hands, and since the removal of these elements would leave a very brief play indeed, it is possible that we have lost some of Marlowe's work. Those who are interested in the textual problems involved can pursue them in the scholarly edition of Sir Walter Greg. For purposes of our criticism, however, it will be sufficient to assume the comparative integrity of the play as it is now usually produced, setting aside any question of authorship and accepting the "comic elements" as parts of a complete play which, whatever the authorship, appeared to be acceptable to the Elizabethan playgoer. Indeed, the additions of buffoonery may indicate a quite lively perception in relation to one aspect of Faustus' damnation. It is no accident that the essential triviality of the bargain for his immortal soul is ironically commented on by the interchange between Wagner and the Clown.

WAGNER
The villain is . . . so hungry, that I know he would give his soul to the devil for a shoulder of mutton, though it were blood-raw.

CLOWN
How! My soul to the devil for a shoulder of mutton, though t'were blood-raw! not so good friend: by'r lady, I had need for it well roasted, and good sauce to it, if I pay so dear.

Whether this inset comic scene were by Marlowe or another hand it is valid comment on the essential triviality of Faustus' commerce with the devil. Nor do the additions greatly affect the very well-wrought shape of the play itself.

It is set within a Prologue and Epilogue which each draw attention to the nature of the tragedy here explored. The Epilogue is wholly unambiguous and with the declaration of moral regret, "cut is the branch that might have grown full straight", the author declares that the play is in series with the late medieval Morality. There is no doubt of the tone nor indeed of the didactic admonition; the audience is exhorted to "regard his hellish fall" in order that a like damnation may be avoided. It is moreover quite clear, as we shall see, that one of the central elements in his damning course is his curiosity which leads him to venture "more than heavenly power permits" Here we confront the essential ambiguity of the Faustian figure from Marlowe to our own day. With the exploratory urge of the Renaissance, curiosity became not a sin but a virtue. Even in Marlowe the exaltation of the scholar figure as he explores new worlds, of thought and of movement, carries overtones of sympathy, despite the fact that it is clear where they tend. In the parallel Polish legend of Pan Twardowski there is an exactly similar exercise of curiosity and a descent into hell, but in this version a momentary penitence in hell achieves its total disappearance, with Pan's restoration to his former standing. In Goethe the conception is naturally even more complex and in the two parts of his *Faust* very varied themes both of learning and of human frailty are inter-related to add a hitherto unachieved density to the subject. Even more ambiguous is the examination of the theme in our own day by Thomas Mann, where curious speculation is recognized as an essential element in combination with the overweening desire for power in the human race, and in particular in the German people. But throughout all these versions the theme is treated ambivalently. Courage, even daring speculation, is accorded approval, and indeed with the growth of scientific speculation pure abstract curiosity, the desire for knowledge for its own sake, becomes a central virtue. At the same time the theological prohibition upon the pursuit of knowledge beyond the bounds which God had set remains an unacknowledged moral factor, producing an unease which tempers our approval for the Faustian figure. It is unnecessary to elaborate the spiritual and psychological strains which the pursuit of atomic fission has imposed on the academic physicist. The extraordinary dilemma is reached whereby knowledge must in conscience be accumulated, while at the same time certain contingent consequences may be appalling.

This dilemma leads us to the brink of a theological crux at which we shall have to look again in examining Milton's *Samson*, namely the doctrine of the "Fortunate Fall". Milton, like Marlowe and some earlier thinkers, was aware that in some respects knowledge and experience achieved even through a fall from grace can be richer and even give rise to such virtues as insight and compassion, beyond the range of primitive, unfallen innocence. There are clearly dangers and latent fallacies in this argument, but there is little doubt that Milton's examination of the accretion of knowledge through the act of the Fall has positive qualities, even considered apart from the argument between Thomist and Scotist on the benefit, derived from the Fall, of the Incarnation of the Son of God. This dilemma is central in Marlowe's *Faustus*.

This play is then at the watershed of medieval and renaissance knowledge. Faustus' opening scene assumes the hierarchy of medieval studies.

> Having commenc'd, be a divine in show.
> Yet level at the end of every art.

It is assumed that a scholar will pass through the full range of logic, philosophy, medicine, law, and the fine arts, until the queen of science, theology is reached. Yet the examination of each stage in this hierarchical pursuit of knowledge is accompanied by an undoubted tone of irony. This critical tone is introduced by an echo of the central temptation set before Eve by Satan, "Ye shall be as gods, knowing . . .". Faustus makes the same querulous assertion,

> Yet art thou still but Faustus and a man . . .
> Here, tire my brains to get a deity . . .

so that his knowledge which is to go beyond divinity will raise him out of the status of humanity, beyond the angelic to the divine. This is not aspiration nor legitimate curiosity, but a presumptuous destruction of the natural order. To go beyond his proper place in nature, a little lower than the angels yet above the beasts in reason, man destroys himself and wrecks due order. This is conveyed in the tone with which he examines his potential studies.

> Philosophy is odious and obscure,
> Both law and physic are for petty wits;
> Divinity is basest of the three,
> Unpleasant, harsh, contemptible, and vile:
> 'Tis magic, magic, that hath ravish'd me.

With this penetrating understanding that knowledge pursued

in this relentless way and with the aid of forbidden arts is damning, Marlowe allies himself with Shakespeare in an echo of Hamlet's ironic characterization of man as "infinite in faculties" yet "a quintessence of dust". This ambivalent quality it is that makes of the massive figure of Leonardo da Vinci, explorer in almost every human faculty, so questionable and central a figure in the Renaissance scene.

When this initial dilemma has been grasped the structure of the play proceeds with clarity. Its core is the Pageant of the Seven Deadly Sins. This achieves many purposes. It sets the tone of the play firmly in the medieval tradition, for the sins are all of them examined in the classical order and manner; it provides an elaborate masque in the centre of the play, which extends far longer in time than the appearance to the reader in the brief text would lead him to suppose; even more important, it provides a standard of orthodoxy in examining the central scenes by which Marlowe's subtle examination of modes outside the orthodox seven can be appreciated and valued. Thus, the tone which Marlowe employs in emphasizing the fall of Faustus is that of levity. For a scholar of distinction, there is a swift and unexamined dismissal of traditional disciplines in the opening scene, which establishes the uncomfortable levity even before the magic arts are conceived. But this is overwhelmingly emphasized in the contrast between the tones of Faustus and Mephistophilis. Faustus is concerned with the status of the damned spirits and with the place of their damnation. This is done in a bogus logical trap concerning the location of hell; the dignity and passion with which Mephistophilis turns aside both the levity and the false logic very effectively places the quality of Faustus' fall.

FAUSTUS
Tell me what is that Lucifer thy Lord?

MEPHISTOPHILIS
Arch-regent and commander of all spirits.

FAUSTUS
Was not that Lucifer an angel once?

MEPHISTOPHILIS
Yes, Faustus, and most dearly lov'd of God.

FAUSTUS
How comes it then that he is Prince of devils?

MEPHISTOPHILIS
O, by aspiring pride and insolence;
For which God threw him from the face of Heaven.

FAUSTUS
And what are you that live with Lucifer?

MEPHISTOPHILIS
Unhappy spirits that fell with Lucifer,
Conspir'd against our God with Lucifer,
And are for ever damn'd with Lucifer.

FAUSTUS
Where are you damn'd?

MEPHISTOPHILIS
In hell.

FAUSTUS
How comes it then that thou art out of hell?

MEPHISTOPHILIS
Why this is hell, nor am I out of it.
Think'st thou that I who saw the face of God,
And tast'd the eternal joys of Heaven,
Am not tormented with ten thousand hells,
In being depriv'd of everlasting bliss?
O Faustus! leave these frivolous demands,
Which strike a terror to my fainting soul.

Equally disturbing is the tone of Faustus' comment upon Helen of Troy. The famous address to Helen suffers from being an anthology piece, and it is not always easy to recognize that the quality addressed is not so much her beauty, certainly not her love, but the destructive element ("burn'd") and the essential lust conveyed not only in the relation between Jupiter and

Semele and in the repetition of words like "wanton", but even more in the slow descent of the passage to the final word "paramour".

> FAUSTUS
> Was this the face that launch'd a thousand ships,
> And burn'd the topless towers of Ilium?
> Sweet Helen make me immortal with a kiss!...
> Oh, thou art fairer than the evening air
> Clad in the beauty of a thousand stars;
> Brighter art thou than flaming Jupiter
> When he appear'd to hapless Semele:
> More lovely than the monarch of the sky
> In wanton Arethusa's azur'd arms:
> And none but thou shalt be my paramour.

(Without suggesting any necessary comparison of value, it is interesting that H. G. Wells makes a similar disturbing relation between boundless power and essential levity in his mythical work, *The Man Who Could Work Miracles*. There was in the film a striking relationship between the newly found miraculous power and the sequence where this power was used solely in the interests of conjuring tricks producing fruit, doves, and other trivial results.)

The point at which our consciousness most radically departs from that of Marlowe's contemporaries lies within that area of illicit knowledge which we know as magic. This is regarded today as either a fearful but remote possibility or non-existent; in the late sixteenth century it was an ever-present possibility. It consisted in attempting to control spirits and even if possible God himself by actions, arts, and formulae so as to serve the private need of those who exercised the magic. It is found in *Faustus* at two levels: at those moments when Faustus delivers his soul to the devil in return for a fixed period of power, a moment which is preceded by the best known of all the exercises of human power, formulae within a magic circle; the second is somewhat concealed, in that it is an exercise in necromancy (the recall of a dead person for illegitimate knowledge), the appearance of Helen of Troy from the dead. Here again, as in the appearance of ghosts in Shakespeare, our scepticism leads us to label moments of this kind as hallucination, where Marlowe's contemporaries would have had no doubt that he was engaged in a damning exercise. The significance of these central moments in the play is that Faustus has now moved right out of his proper and customary intellectual pursuits. The honourable ascent through the hierarchy of the university is abandoned, and he engages wholeheartedly in a course of power and knowledge to which man is not permitted to aspire. This then is the culmination of that curiosity which, as we have already seen, is a central sin in this play.

The ultimately damning element in *Dr. Faustus* is the total reversal of values into which he is led. The cry, "Evil be thou my good", has been the universal assumption of demonic power, but in this play Marlowe uses a very skilful literary device in order to place it vividly in the contemporary mind. At the powerful and tragic moment when Faustus signs away his soul, he does so in the form of a bond which must be signed and sealed. Nature conspires with the powers of good to arrest the evil in his course; his blood in which he was to sign the bond congeals and the charcoal fire has to be deliberately and wilfully employed in order that the signature may be appended. This is sufficiently harrowing to the spectator, but a further turn is given to the tragic evil. As Faustus signs the bond the flourish is accompanied by the words:

> Consummatum est: this bill is ended,
> And Faustus hath bequeathed his soul to Lucifer.

The blasphemous irony of this phrase would be immediately apparent to Marlowe's audience; Faustus is signing away his soul with the last words of Christ on the Cross by which he declares that his redeeming power for human souls has been

fulfilled and made available. A yet further irony is reserved for
the end of the play, and since the medium is again a Latin
quotation, it is inevitably related to this first moment of irony.
In the agony with which Faustus approaches his final end he
cries:

O lente, lente, currite noctis equi,

in which, in a quotation from Ovid's *Amores*, he prays in the
words of a lover that the hours of the night may be extended.
So, at one moment, he destroys his soul with words of redemption and at the end of his magic powers he clings to his soul's
life with words of licentiousness. Marlowe's dramatic art
reaches no higher point of ironic insight.

The one sin for which there can be no redemption is that of
despair. Faustus' career begins with an assertion of pride, that
he shall be more than man with something approximating to
omniscience. When this pattern has fulfilled its course the only
mode left to him is despair of his own powers, and tragically
this leads to despair of grace itself. The close of this final and
greatest Morality is a descent into hell's mouth in which all the
agony of seeing the possibility of redemption—

See, see where Christ's blood streams in the firmament!—

is denied by his inability to clutch at grace. The very word
"streams", with its suggestion of the flowing of blood and the
extension of a banner through the sky, asserts the triumphant
possibilities denied by the malignant forces that drag him to
hell. Medieval art has here reached its final and highest point,
and the way is now open for the triumph of secular drama.

4

Shakespeare

There is much substance in the judgement that Marlowe's work, especially in *Dr. Faustus*, carries at least as much medieval matter and formal tone as of modern attitudes, that in fact his work is a true watershed. Yet it would be a dangerous assumption that assumed Shakespeare, his successor, to be moving firmly and completely into the modern consciousness. We shall see in a consideration of Jonson and Tourneur that the dramatists conservatively carried over much of the temper of medieval thinking, and it is a nice exercise in discrimination to see those points in his drama in which Shakespeare is either clearly exploring new ways of thought or basing his analysis of character and situation upon traditional moral and theological assumptions. This, moreover, involves us more sharply than hitherto in our examination of religious drama in the main critical dilemma of relating the thought structure and the tone of a play to the personal beliefs of the dramatist. If we tease out, on our reading or enjoyment of the play in theatre, the elements which are in fact inextricably bound together, namely the characterization, the plot and theme, and the image patterns, we find in fact that we subtly shift our own interpretation of the impact of the play as we give greater or less attention to these three elements in turn. It is manifest that in the creation of characters who have their own integrity within the

universe of the play a dramatist endows them with their own
appropriate beliefs and attitudes, and it would be imprudent
critical method to attribute any degree of these attitudes to the
author. To attribute Edmund's Machiavellian paganism,
Henry V's pieties, or Hamlet's casuistic examination of motives
severally to Shakespeare would be to reduce the dramatic act
to nonsense. The second element, the pattern of plot and
theme, clearly moves into more conceptual considerations
which must involve the relation of the author's opinions to the
prevailing intellectual climate of his day. But, as a substantial
area of critical practice has demonstrated during the past
thirty years, the image pattern and clusters in the work of the
dramatist reveal both conscious and unconscious attitudes to
the great abstractions of his day, the political, social, cosmo-
logical, religious, and moral areas of speculation which colour
the tendency of the play. One critical task therefore is the
delicate assessment of these attitudes, the degree of assent to
prevailing orthodoxies, and the departure into tentative exploratory speculation, within single plays or groups. Thus it is
on occasion invaluable to consider a play by Shakespeare not in
isolation but, with careful safeguards, in relation to others in a
roughly defined group, his History plays, the so-called Dark
Comedies or Problem group, the central tragedies, or that relatively sharply defined closing movement of his work which
we now neutrally label simply the Last Plays. Each period or
group appears to have its own peculiar problems, even though
these exist in continuity throughout his work and though there
may be modulation and clarification within and across these
groups. It is my conviction that in no field of religious drama is
discriminating criticism of theological values more vital than
in our consideration of Shakespeare's work, if we are to see the
full intellectual interplay of religious speculation and the
theatre.

A further important check on our criticism is given by our

knowledge of the intellectual attitudes of his contemporaries; these provide the limits of orthodoxy and, with whatever allowance we make for "genius", the rough limits also of eccentric speculation. The drama of Shakespeare is the near-contemporary of the writings of Donne, Andrewes, and Herbert; within his lifetime there were important re-statements of Neoplatonic philosophy, of Machiavellian statecraft, of Calvinist and recusant theology, in addition to the prevailing orthodoxy of the established Church. There was, moreover, blurring the edges of politics and theology, the regular use of that most ambiguous of Stuart terms, "atheism". The close-knit, quite small community of early seventeenth-century London with its concentration of intellect in courtly circles, the Inns of Court, the Church, the theatre, and the diverse communities of the arts, produced an intellectual liveliness and variety of attitude which the drama of the period in particular reflected.

Shakespeare's History plays provide us with a convenient starting-point for considering the prevailing relation of the social order to the great speculations concerning the physical universe and man's place within it. One of the great commonplaces to which a vast amount of attention has been devoted is that of the relation of the "little world of man", the microcosm of the human body or of the city or State, to the great world of the created universe, the macrocosm which God established in a hierarchical order. As man occupied a significant central position in this hierarchy, below the angels, yet participating in their reason, and above the beasts, yet participating in their nature, so the King within the State occupied a status of central significance both as God's vicegerent and as the head of the body politic. The divinity that hedges a king, his unremitting responsibility, and the tragic disparity between his status and the essential human fallibility of his person, provides a central

theme in Shakespeare's History plays. The tension of status and
person is in fact a prevailing tragic fact through both the histories and the tragedies, and can be fully understood only in a
theological context which goes beyond any merely moral
evaluation of kingly action. The closest analogy is the canonical
dictum that the unworthiness of a minister in no way invali-
dates his sacramental ministry. The status of a priest or a king
may correspond, with gracious consequences, to his personal
qualities; there may, with tragic consequences be a total disparity between the two. Our judgement of Richard II, of Prince
Hal, of Wolsey, inevitably shifts between reprehension of their
inadequacy for the status they hold and compassion for their
human failing. Hooker expresses most fully the weight, both
of status and of expectation, imposed upon a monarch at the
very rite of coronation:

> Crowned we see they are, and enthroned, and anointed; the
> crown a sign of military, the throne of judicial and oil of religious
> power.

This union of complex status and function within a person
who is merely human focuses the dilemma of the universal
status of man as a creature. Hamlet's antithesis of awe before
the dignity of this "piece of work", in so many aspects "so
express and admirable" and his quality as "quintessence of
dust" is a central statement of the human standing. This
examination of the character problem is theologically reinforced by the Tudor and Stuart reinterpretation of history
itself. Throughout the Middle Ages and indeed up to the
threshold of Shakespeare's writing, the prevailing mode of
history had been annalistic, the simple record of event with
comparatively little interpretation. The development of
Tudor history-making which reaches its consummation in
Shakespeare's theatre enlarges and clarifies the providential
element within the actions of history; events are under the

hand of God. The fulfilment of this providential interpretation of history is found in that work which is probably one of Shakespeare's last, *King Henry VIII*. In the closing scene the infant Elizabeth is baptized and Cranmer expresses prophetically a conclusion in her reign of God's historic intention. The language not only echoes Old Testament rhythms but specifically quotes the Psalmist's intuition that Israel is the vine planted in a good ground:

> In her days every man shall eat in safety,
> Under his own vine, what he plants, and sing
> The merry songs of peace to all his neighbours:
> God shall be truly known; and those about her
> From her shall read the perfect ways of honour,
> And by those claim their greatness.

Very much earlier in his dramatic course, Shakespeare had given an equally precise examination of providential shaping when, at the opening *King Henry V*, Hal is transmuted to a king in both status and person.

> The breath no sooner left his father's body,
> But that his wildness, mortified in him,
> Seem'd to die too; yea, at that very moment,
> Consideration like an angel came
> And whipp'd the offending Adam out of him,
> Leaving his body as a paradise,
> To envelop and contain celestial spirits,

in which the prevailing image of Fall and redemption is precisely related to the stature of kingship.

The tragedies maintain the perspectives of history if only to the degree that they are again concerned with order and hierarchy. But they cannot be confined to this dimension. *Julius Caesar* examines the central tragedy of the secular world, focal in that sphere as the Incarnation is central in the religious sphere. *King Lear* provides a more mature analysis of the human situation. Lear's relation with his daughters and with Cordelia in particular is a paradigm of the total ambiguity of our personal commitments, in claims upon each other and in compassionate insight. His question concerning the *quantity* of love and its blasphemous relationship to a graded reward is intensified by the further blasphemy of his response to Cordelia, "Nothing will come of nothing", which denies the miraculous nature of the created order itself and of the creative miracle of human love. Out of this disorder (and the parallel disorder of Gloucester's relationship with his sons) arises the profounder disorder in Lear's mind and the related chaos in the elements. The third and fourth acts provide our gravest difficulties in interpretation; the tempest on the heath can be read as in some way a pathetic fallacy, a mere correspondence between mind and external nature. In fact Lear's words deny this limited relationship; the tempest in his mind has a relationship to the disordered universe which is an analogue to the Fall itself, by which, in St Paul's words, the whole creation is involved in the tragedy and awaits, with man, the redemptive power of Christ. Lear's heath, moreover, carries overtones both of the first deluge and of a final cataclysm which will

> Strike flat the thick rotundity o' th' world.

The final summary of this tragic moment in the play is to be found in Albany's comment, that if the heavens do not intervene to right the disorder in both man and nature,

> It will come,
> Humanity must perforce prey upon itself
> Like monsters of the deep.

The conclusion of the play has the spiritual ambiguity of all high tragedy in that the problem is faced, in action if not in interpretation, of a common retribution falling upon guilty and relatively innocent alike. At their impending inprisonment,

Lear and Cordelia achieve a renewed radiance of relationship: they will reach a mutual blessing and forgiveness. Yet this is followed by the tragedy of Cordelia's hanging, of Lear's broken heart, and of the muted acceptance of a tragic future even by Edgar, the restored kingly successor. We are left at the conclusion of the play with the profound intuition that there is neither rational explanation nor any mitigation in this tragic view of life, but that the impact of the play's nobility leads to a sense of exaltation.

This is not the tragic mode of *Macbeth*. This, to adopt Eliot's words, is a story "of sin and expiation"; under the impact of demonic powers Macbeth overthrows the divinely established order, nature responds in the fearful images of the very horses devouring each other, and in the comparative order of an armed castle a servant finds himself almost literally "porter of hell gate". If this were then to become a story of expiation alone we should find in it little more than the materials of French classical tragedy. It is, however, an exploration, shaded with complex ironies, not only of even-handed justice but of a descent of the sinning soul into an appalling negation. The theme of purgation is outlined with dramatic simplicity in the ironic relation of two speeches by Lady Macbeth: after the murder she assumes with spiritual levity that "A little water clears us of this deed"; yet at the conclusion of her tragedy, her agony is concentrated in the question, "What, will these hands ne'er be clean?". Yet even this irony falls short of that aspect of hell to which Macbeth enters, which is so close to the perception of Mephistophilis, that absence of the beatific vision is the essence of damnation. Macbeth's examination of his own life as it draws to its close concludes with the judgement:

> It is a tale
> Told by an idiot, full of sound and fury
> Signifying nothing.

Though tragedy is so frequently given graver attention than a dramatist's comedies, Shakespeare showed a unique variety in his handling of the comic mode. In the early comedies his happiest intuitions are directed towards resolving the problems which lie between the sexes. *The Taming of the Shrew* appeared to take a short way with the problem and Katharine concludes with an elaborate assertion of a woman's subordination in a natural hierarchy of values. But in the maturer comedies of *As You Like It* and *Twelfth Night* traditional insights deepen the gaiety of their conclusions; thus, *As You Like It* opens by examining the relations of Orlando to his brother in terms of the parable of the Prodigal Son, glanced at in a brief phrase: "Shall I keep your hogs, and eat husks? . . . What prodigal portion have I spent? . . . Give me the poor allottery my father left me by testament." Similarly Viola in *Twelfth Night*, in the dilemma of her love, falls back upon a providential view of life: "Time, thou must untangle this not I." These overtones of theology and the scriptures are echoed most profoundly not in his drama but in his greatest metaphysical poem, where the relationships of human love are made explicable only in terms of relationships within the Blessed Trinity, the mutual relation of two persons in human love reflecting those relations within the Triune Godhead.

> So they lov'd as love in twain
> Had the essence but in one.
> Two distincts, division none;
> Number there in love was slain,

an expression as terse as that of the Athanasian Creed.

The range of comedy is greatly extended in those which we instinctively call "Dark". They are prefigured by the sombre trial scene of the *Merchant of Venice*, which in its turn anticipates the tragic farce of Lear's trial of the joint-stool in his hovel on the heath; but the theme of justice and its relation to equity and compassion is seen at its most profound in *Measure for*

Measure. Angelo, who can be seduced from virtue only by desire for a being of the highest beauty and integrity, warps for her sake all the processes of human justice, and is led to a contrition of tragic intensity when, faced with his condition, he pleads for his own overthrow:

> No longer session hold upon my shame,
> But let my trial be mine own confession:
> Immediate sentence then, and sequent death,
> Is all the grace I beg.

In its own noble manner this has analogies with that other intuition reached by the ignoble Parolles:

> Even the thing I am shall make me live.

Here the response to the moral exaltation, "Man, know thyself", raises even a creature of this quality to a degree of insight which focuses the relationship of the two principal characters, Bertram and Helena.

The Last Plays have given rise to considerable speculative criticism. At certain periods of romantic interpretation they were regarded as light romances in the manner of Fletcher. They are now accorded the greater justice which has come from a realization that they are united by common themes of redemption and of "Losing and Finding". *The Tempest* is manifestly related, in its use of chaotic imagery, to the tragic tempests of Lear and Othello. Prospero's serenity, his abjuring magic arts, and his return to authority in Milan carries with it a new-found innocence in the love of Miranda. *The Winter's Tale* borders still more nearly upon the insights of tragedy; indeed, two deaths are part of the price of the ultimate radiance. As so often with Shakespeare the tragic action is centred upon a trial, and out of its manifest injustice there comes the sixteen-years alienation of Leontes and Hermione. Once more, youthful innocence in the person of Perdita through a splendid evocation of the pastoral tradition in Act IV achieves the final reconciliation. In Paulina's revelation of the apparently dead Hermione death and gracious life are set against each other.

> Bequeath to death your numbness, for from him
> Dear life redeems you.

This is extended in the punning phrase, "Our Perdita is found" which recollects the parables of the sheep, the coin, and the son. The spiritual insights of this closing scene are locked in a final perception of the significance of flesh itself; Hermione is not only restored after long interval to her husband; his breathing wonder, "O, she's warm!", expresses the awed delight in the restoration of flesh itself.

The body of Shakespeare's plays is, it need not be stressed, a structure for the theatre; it is no dramatic theology, but its structure is integrated by the credal assumptions of his age, and its temper breathes by the devotional insights of the seventeenth century.

5

Shakespeare's Contemporaries

It is clearly difficult to make generalized judgements about the moral or theological content of the dramatic output of even one man. We have seen that modes of insight and of theological expression vary very greatly over the span of Shakespeare's work; so varied was the output of his contemporaries, in the richest period of English drama that it would be rash in the extreme to attribute to them any strict uniformity of attitude. There is clearly a vast difference in the approach to social problems between the "bourgeois" dramatists like Dekker and the intensely conservative Ben Jonson. *The Shoemaker's Holiday* praises very properly the social mobility of an increasingly self-conscious artisan class; *Volpone* on the other hand brings to bear a positively medieval astringency on matters which in an earlier age would have been called usury. None the less the bulk of these leading dramatists writing between the closing years of Elizabeth's reign and the mid-twenties of the seventeenth century, whatever their personal orthodoxy, had a certain pattern of assumptions which perpetuated into the new age the attitudes and beliefs which we have seen survive from the medieval Morality into the theatre of Marlowe.

Ben Jonson is for this purpose a central figure. His characterization based on the theory of humours has very complex affinities. In the first place, it assumes a late medieval system of "correspondences", with the elements of the physical

universe, earth, air, fire, and water corresponding to the con-
stitutents in our bodies which control the make-up of our
character, namely phlegm, choler, bile, and black bile; since
each individual "in his humour" falls into certain categories—
which look alarmingly like some of the categories into which
our present psychological theories place individuals—these will
have a tendency to convey moral judgement and to approach
very closely to the figures of Morality drama. What begins
then as a psychological account of man's character carries
overtones of dramatic judgement some of which can clearly be
seen to survive in our own descriptions of individuals as
"choleric" or "phlegmatic". Ben Jonson's two Humour plays
indicate quite clearly his moral-satiric attitudes, but these are
sharpened very considerably in such a play as *The Alchemist*
where greed and hypocrisy are associated in a common satiric
analysis. Epicure Mammon is a major study in the greed which
the new-found attitudes reinforced in England, but he is a great
deal more than that; his exaltation of the values of the flesh and
his hypocrisy are related in a calculated inflation of language
which anticipates the highest moments of *Volpone*. At the same
time the puritan figures Ananias and Tribulation Wholesome
clarify the attitudes of an essentially conservative mind towards the new sectarianism while the dramatic substratum of
the whole play is a convincingly accurate account of both the
science and the charlatanry of alchemy.

Volpone, however, is Ben Jonson's masterpiece in this mode of
the critical analysis of moral attitudes. Its satire on greed and
the breakdown of the old sanctions on usurious activities is conducted with the utmost economy. Volpone, the vulpine creature, is surrounded by characters who are all of them birds of
prey, so that judgements are conducted with an even greater
limitation of means than in the categories of medieval drama.

There is a sharp contrast between the quality of this highly
intellectual drama and the more popular Morality of the

"revenge dramatists". John Webster is the subtlest exponent of this mode but its complexity is perhaps best exemplified by Tourneur's *Revenger's Tragedy*.

T. S. Eliot has said of this work:

> The play is a document on humanity chiefly because it is a document on one human being, Tourneur; its motive is truly the death motive, for it is the loathing and horror of life itself. To have realised this motive so well is a triumph; for the hatred of life is an important phase—even is, if you like, a mystical experience—in life itself.

This statement gives rational expression to the curious uncertainty which a reader feels on first reading the play; it is clearly a work of high seriousness, it is pervaded by an obvious moral purpose, and yet there is a repellent morbidity in its tone, a feeling of moral sickness even at the moments when it appears most didactic. If this is felt to express "loathing of life itself", it seems to be an ambiguous candidate for the class "religious drama". Yet without in any way straining the meaning of either term, "revenge plays", of which this is one of the most distinguished examples, by their form and intention, demand examination as "religious drama"; they are in fact one of the most important extensions of religious dramatic writing from the medieval into the Elizabethan period.

The very great popularity of the revenge play in the Elizabethan theatre cannot be wholly accounted for either by the power of Seneca as a literary influence nor by the demand of the popular theatre for the "drama of blood". Kyd, Chapman, Marson, Webster, Tourneur, and Shakespeare, all practised the form with distinction (*Hamlet* sets us some of the most perplexing problems in the whole revenge tradition) and this serious preoccupation by the greatest dramatists belies any easy appeal to theatrical fashion.

A more attractive solution is that this type of play answered in dramatic terms to the Jacobean passion for law. The universal concern to recognize the operation of law, divine, natural, and positive, pervaded the drama, revealing itself in the frequent trial scenes and the constant dramatic conclusion in judgement, legal and moral. Revenge may be interpreted as an individual's seizing upon the instruments of retribution; it is, in Bacon's phrase, "wild justice"—though Bacon, as a good lawyer, deplores its exercise: "revenge of wrong putteth the law out of office".

Webster is especially interesting in this concern for law. His two best-known plays, *The Duchess of Malfi* and *The White Devil*, have all the characteristics of revenge plays; *The Devil's Law Case*, for all its sardonic wit, employs at a vital point in the plot a tag from Hooker's *Ecclesiastical Polity*: "Obedience of creatures to the law of nature is the stay of the whole world." Indeed, no simple judgement on the moral nature of revenge as the Elizabethans conceived it appears possible. At the level of vendetta it would seem a crude realization of the *lex talionis*, "an eye for an eye"; in the universal condemnation of the person of the revenger in these plays the revenge tradition in the Elizabethan theatre appears to fulfil the divine command: "Vengeance is mine: I will repay, saith the Lord."

A further complication is introduced by the relationship which the person of the revenger has to the plot. In one group of plays, the prototype of which is the Senecan *Spanish Tragedy* of Kyd, the revenge is always carried out by a blood relation; here a father avenges his son's murder; in *Hamlet* a son is to avenge his father. Senecan stoicism, with its stress on the universality of the moral law, is an appropriate intellectual background to this form of the tragedy, and it accords well with certain aspects of the Elizabethan realization of the providential handling of sin, that God works out in time and nature the consequences of guilt. In the second group of plays the revenger is hired, has no blood relationship with the injured victim but is usually conceived in terms of Machiavellian

villainy. The finest example of this second type is Webster's
Duchess of Malfi, in which the dubious motives of the Duke and
Cardinal for avenging themselves on their sister the Duchess
are reflected in the morbid villainy of Bosola the revenger, one
of the most complex studies in Elizabethan drama. One of the
peculiar interests of *The Revenger's Tragedy* is that it unites
these two themes in a moral struggle of particular subtlety
and intensity. For Vindice is at once a hired Machiavellian and
involved in the closest blood ties with those on whom he has to
exact vengeance; the opportunity for tragic irony in this
situation is not neglected.

Tourneur's intuitive response to life may be "suffering,
cynicism and despair" but with his reasoning mind he realizes
and gives the dramatic form to a sane moral order. For there is
something of the directness of a morality play in the dramatic
statement of the characters. Their names—Lussurioso, Castiza,
Spurio, Gratiana, Vindice—reduce the complexity of their relationships to a symbolic pattern. Yet there are stresses in the
play which threaten both to destroy the plot and expand the
character-symbolism to breaking point; for there is a constant
shifting of tone between moral judgement and depravity. In
the first act Lussurioso tests Vindice's quality as his potential
instrument:

LUSSURIOSO
Fine villain! troth, I like him wondrously:
He's e'en shaped for my purpose.
                    Then thou know'st
I'th' world strange lust!

VINDICE
O Dutch lust! fulsome lust!
. . . O hour of incest!
Any kin now, next to the rim o'th' sister
Is men's meat in these days; and in the morning,
When they are up and dressed, and their mask on,
Who can perceive this, save that eternal eye,
That sees through flesh and all?

The sudden shift to the assertion of judgement in "that eternal eye" is disconcerting after the apparent gloating with which Vindice shares in the prospect of "strange lust". This rapid transition from depravity to moral judgement is used with the reverse effect in a later speech by Lussurioso:

> I'll trust thee in the business of my heart
> Because I see thee well experienced.
> In this luxurious day wherein we breathe
> Go thou, and with a smooth enchanting tongue
> Bewitch her ears, and cosen her of all grace:
> Enter upon the portion of her soul—
> Her honour, which she calls her chastity,
> And bring it into expense.

Here the perception of the horror of "this luxurious day wherein we breathe", which lies behind Tourneur's sceptical loathing, is intensified by being so strangely involved with theological terminology. The phrase "portion of her soul" (an echo of the "portions" of Jacob and of the Prodigal Son) is a recognition of the essential grace and purity of Castiza which stands in perpetual opposition to the impious lechery of Lussurioso.

This tension of opposites, however, not only adds to the cynical tone of the play but preserves a tenuous moral standard. There is a continuous reference to the opposition between the virtues of the country and the vices of the court:

> That nobleman has been i'th' country, for he does not lie

or in the ironic:

> Live wealthy, rightly understand the world,
> And chide away that foolish country girl
> Keeps company with your daughter—Chastity

which is contrasted with the character of the court mistress:

> A drab of state, a cloth-o'-silver slut,
> To have her train borne up and her soul trail i' the dust.

But in spite of this continuous moral censorship, critics constantly find in Tourneur's tragedy evidence of "diseased per-

versity and crippled nobleness". J. A. Symonds declares that
Vindice reveals Tourneur's cynical scepticism: "In the strongest
scene of the play he showed his scorpion of revenge, stooping
to feign a pander's part, tempting his mother and his sister as
none but a moral leper could have done." But this is only half
the story. Vindice's asides during the temptation of his mother
and sister on Lussurioso's behalf make it dramatically quite
clear that his intention is to secure assurance of their virtuous
constancy:

>   I will lay
> Hard siege to my mother, though I know
> A syren's tongue could not bewitch her so.

As his stratagem appears to find success with his mother, he
cries:

> O suffering Heaven, with thy invisible finger,
> E'en at this instant turn the precious side
> Of both mine eyeballs inward not to see myself.

His deliberate self-torture as he pursues Lussurioso's ends is
heightened by the ironic levity of Castiza as she realizes her
mother's degradation:

> I cry you mercy! Lady I mistook you!
> Pray did you see my mother? which way went you?
> Pray God I have not lost her.

The scene ends, not with cynicism, but with a strong repre-
sentation of sin and a despairing desire that the moral order be
vindicated:

> Why does not Heaven turn black, or with a frown
> Undo the world? Why does not earth start up,
> And strike the sins that tread upon't?

Later the vindication is forthcoming and at Gratiana's tears of
repentance Vindice exclaims:

> I' faith, 'tis a sweet shower, it does much good.
> The fruitful grounds and meadows of her soul
> Have been long dry; pour down thou blessed dew!

and in Gratiana's reply there is an interesting reinforcement of this tone by an oblique reference to the preparation of holy water with salt:

> O you Heavens! take this infectious spot out of my soul,
> I'll rinse it in seven waters of mine eyes!
> Make my ears salt enough to taste of grace.

From this point to the end the correct gestures of retribution and even of penitence are made. Order and law are reasserted ("Just is the law above") and even-handed justice disposes of all the depraved agents of the plot. Antonio, the nobleman of "reverend years", will make

> . . . the silver age again
> When there were fewer but more honest men

and there is a measure of innocent restoration. Yet in spite of this seemly ending one is left with the uneasy question whether a world so corrupt could be redeemed in the mind of one who felt its corruption with such a mordant sympathy. The mind of the dramatist moves along the traditional way of penitential purgation but his senses are committed to the rank decadence.

6

Milton: *Samson Agonistes*

Milton wrote *Samson Agonistes* towards the end of his life and it was published with *Paradise Regained* in 1671, although completed a few years earlier. It cannot be treated apart from *Paradise Lost* and *Paradise Regained* for it attempts to "justify the ways of God to men" in a particular situation, as the epic treats the general problem of sin, free will, and redemption.

This is Milton's attempt at the second major classical form, the tragedy. His early drafts of the theme of *Paradise Lost* were also in the form of a classical tragedy, for he felt it a moral obligation to write a Christian poem in literary forms which were classical achievements of the human imagination—even though their earlier exponents, Homer, Aeschylus, Sophocles, Euripides, had been denied the grace of the Christian revelation. *Samson Agonistes* obeys the Aristotelian canons, for Milton shared the Renaissance respect for Aristotle's observations, which came to be regarded as inviolable rules. His prefatory note, "Of that sort of Dramatic Poem which is called Tragedy", opens with his tribute to the Aristotelian canons:

> Tragedy, as it was anciently compos'd, hath been ever held the gravest, moralest, and most profitable of all other Poems: therefore said by Aristotle to be of power by raising pity and fear, or terror, to purge the mind of these and such like passions—that is, to temper and reduce them to just measure with a kind of delight, stirr'd up by reading or seeing those passions well imitated.

The "unities" are observed in Samson but the unity of time is imaginatively used to point the contrast between Samson's former power and his present helplessness, "eyeless in Gaza at the mill with slaves"; similarly the Chorus is not just a mechanical classical device but is fluidly used to play a variety of rôles in the drama. Sometimes its members speak as a group of Samson's intimate friends and are as human and individual as the women of Canterbury in Murder in the Cathedral; often, like Job's visitors, they reflect in general terms, or, like the Fool in Lear, give comment that is objective, yet not aloof from the tragic drama. The great moments in Samson are the hymn-like affirmations of the Chorus, when Milton's verse is more direct and austere than previously, but as evocative as any rhetorical and allusive paragraph in Paradise Lost. In Samson too it is possible to detect an urgency in the verse that had not been present or even desirable in the other work; in the play it was not only demanded by the dramatic form but invoked also by a natural sympathy for the theme: a former champion rendered useless, unable to serve his nation, blind and dependent, yet, like Job, forced to meditate on the justice of Providence. Yet Samson Agonistes is not a "psychological release" for Milton; his attitude to his own blindness was courageously positive, as the conclusion of his sonnet shows (like many of Donne's sonnets, this is a formal meditation, with a question posed for exploration and answer, which gives it a poised objectivity), but we can legitimately feel that Milton's peculiar insight into Samson's tragedy gives power to the work, when, formally speaking, it is in danger of being static.

The story of Samson is swiftly and simply told in the Book of Judges, with no pointing of the moral and little indication of any change in Samson himself, his final concern being to "be at once avenged of the Philistines for my two eyes" (Judges 16.28), but tradition had seen in Samson a repetition of the primal weakness of Adam in yielding to his wife, and in

Delilah the type of seductive, fundamentally unloving, and treacherous woman (the Hollywood treatment of her character went no further, in spite of glamorization, than her regular rôle in medieval *exempla* or the secular diatribes of that age against women). Unlike the biblical version there is clear pointing of the moral in Milton, and sometimes it is even inartistically underlined. The "temptation" theme was a favourite with Milton; *Comus*, with the Enchanter's temptation of the Lady; the temptation of Eve by Satan; of Adam by Eve; and, a disquieting culmination, in *Paradise Regained*, for its central action is the temptation of Christ by Satan, an antitype of the action in the Fall, and his victory over temptation is regarded as the moment of redemption, set apart from the Cross and Resurrection. In *Samson Agonistes*, Dalila returns to tempt him and this is the dramatic turning-point; Samson has already achieved wisdom and can speak of his former failure:

> [I] like a foolish pilot, have shipwrecked
> My vessel trusted to me from above,
> Gloriously rigged, and for a word, a tear

where there is a recollection of the New Testament use of "vessel" ("know how to possess his vessel in sanctification and honour"). When Dalila enters, her attraction is conveyed in a simile that recalls Samson's earlier confession, and extends the pun on "vessel":

> [She] bedecked, ornate, and gay,
> Comes this way sailing,
> Like a stately ship
> Of Tarsus, bound for the isles
> Of Javan and Gadire,
> With all her bravery on, and tackle trim,
> Sails filled and streamers waving,
> Courted by all the winds that hold them play;
> An amber scent of odorous perfume
> Her harbinger, a damsel train behind.

This conveys her voluptuous quality as vividly as Van Dyck's painting in the Dulwich Gallery, London, and this picture is worth examining for a moment, as a comparison with Milton's treatment. Painted some time before 1620, this is a relatively young man's work. Dramatically it is brilliantly organized. To the left, half-withdrawn behind a pillar, a group of armed Philistines wait for the overwhelmed Samson; balancing them on the right two female servants, a young woman horrified by the impending tragedy and an old woman horridly and curiously impassive, bend over Delilah's shoulder; the greater part of the canvas is occupied by a massive triangle: a half-naked Samson lies with a voluptuous curved body, helpless for the shearing, above a dark and mature figure leans over him, grasping his hair to be severed by large and clumsy sheep shears, the group completed by Delilah clothed in a shimmering blue satin and gazing on the fall of Samson with an ambiguous union of curiosity, lust, and determination. Here, in a static picture there is a fully baroque drama, extending in the tensions of the composition and moral implications of the tragedy.

In Milton's drama Samson is only partly seen as a tragic hero in the classical sense because he stresses that the cause of his fall is wilful sin, stronger than the "tragic flaw" of classical drama. Nevertheless he meditates on his downfall in Aristotelian fashion, on "what once I was and what am now", an aspect of his tragedy taken up in the first speech of the Chorus:

> Can this be he,
> That heroic, that renowned
> Irresistible Samson? . . .
> By how much from the top of wondrous glory,
> Strongest of mortal men,
> To lowest pitch of abject fortune thou are fallen!

Manoa echoes this theme more poignantly, recalling his auspicious birth and former triumphs. By the Chorus, Samson's double misery is movingly pictured:

> Which shall I first bewail
> Thy bondage or lost sight,
> Prison within prison
> Insuperably dark?
> Thou art become (O worst imprisonment!)
> The dungeon of thyself; thy soul
> (Which men enjoying sight oft without cause complain)
> Imprisoned now indeed,
> In real darkness of the body dwells.

Samson himself speaks of his "*dark* steps" and the word becomes a cry of anguish in its bald reiteration:

> O dark, dark, dark amid the blaze of noon,
> Irrecoverably dark, total eclipse,
> Without all hope of day!

But Samson's darkness is not simply physical; his thoughts are "black mortification" and his weakness a moral blindness, "servile mind / Rewarded well with servile punishment". Milton shows the return of Samson's inward vision and moral strength, so that his already recovered physical strength can be used to the glory of God, and, like Gloucester in *King Lear* (anticipated by Oedipus), he too can acknowledge that he stumbled when he saw. His attitude becomes something greater than stoical fortitude or the patience which he does not desire.

> Unless he feel within
> Some source of consolation from above,
> Secret refreshings that repair his strength.

It is his patience, the "exercise of saints", which attempts to realize the "new acquist / Of true experience from this great event".

These two aspects of Milton's treatment of the subject—the examination of the individual tragedy of Samson, and the *exemplum* of his weakness in temptation—interweave with his larger concern, to emphasize the justice of Providence. At the end of *Paradise Lost*, Michael shows Adam visions of both the consequence of his sin, the disruptive, destructive effect of Satan's domination, and the creative, positive, and loving action of God, continually making good out of evil (the reverse of Satan's ambition). Indeed, the teasing relationship between the Fall and new powers granted to man in God's providence, enshrined theologically in the ambiguous phrase, "the doctrine of the fortunate Fall", achieves one of its most complex expressions in the closing lines of *Paradise Lost*. In the Thomist system the cry "O felix culpa!" expressed the intuition that the Incarnation was God's providential instrument for meeting and correcting the sin of man, it was a "happy", even a "blessed" fault ("beata culpa") which would herald the birth of the Son of God. But *Paradise Lost* looks forward to no such distant bliss in its closing lines; it is true that paradise was lost, that the Gate of Paradise was thronged with "dreadful Faces" and with "fierie Armes". But Adam and Eve moved out of their patrimony with muted tragedy:

> Som natural tears they drop'd, but wip'd them soon;
> The World was all before them, where to choose
> Thir place of rest, and Providence thir guide.

Samson Agonistes also develops this theme, for Milton interprets the story as many Jewish and Elizabethan writers interpreted history. Samson's downfall is seen to be a consequence of sin, of disobedience and uxorious weakness, but in spite of this God's pattern of providence subsists and persists. Yet the problem is not facilely answered, nor is the movement of thought continually ascending. After the affirmation of the Chorus:

> Just are the ways of God
> And justifiable to men,

the problem of the apparent rejection of the *elect* remains, of God's seeming levity in giving Samson physical strength without corresponding spiritual stature, and throughout there is a probing of this mystery by the Chorus as well as by Samson:

> God of our fathers, what is Man
> That thou towards him with a hand so various
> Or might I say contrarious,
> Temperest thy Providence through his short course,
> Not evenly, as thou rul'st
> The angelic orders and inferior creatures mute,
> Irrational and brute . . .
> Nor do I name of men the common rout . . .
> But such as thou most solemnly elected.

Samson answers this question, for it is man who is "contrarious"; God is not only just but merciful, and "all is best", for God does not desert his "faithful champion" but "bears witness gloriously". Samson himself learns not resignation but fresh courage; he is no longer guilty of despair, and gives a proper answer to Harapha, resolved now

> Nothing to do, be sure, that may dishonour
> Our law, or stain my vow of Nazarite.
> Happen what may, of me expect to hear
> Nothing dishonourable, impure, unworthy
> Of God, our Law, my nation or myself.

This renewal is commented upon by the Semichorus, using the traditional image of the phoenix:

> So Virtue, given for lost,
> Depressed and overthrown, as seemed,
> Like that self-begotten bird . . .
> Revives, reflourishes, then vigorous most
> When most inactive deemed.

Samson Agonistes is religious drama in two senses: Milton presents the theme with a faithfulness to the bibilical text and a moral point that is characteristic of the miracle plays or directly evangelistic drama; but he also poses, and answers dramatically, questions that are asked in all great drama,

whether the author is a Christian like Eliot, a pagan like
Sophocles, or an unbeliever like Anouilh. The questions grow
out of the material; the dilemma *is* the dramatic situation and
the depth of the statement as well as the resolution is a
measure of greatness.

The story of Samson was pursued through the next two centuries both in art and literature, and it is instructive to compare
two treatments by Blake at the end of the eighteenth and the
beginning of the nineteenth century with those of Van Dyck
and Milton in the seventeenth. In the little-read but interesting
fragment of a prose-poem, Blake opens with a double echo, of
Virgil and Milton:

> Samson, the strongest of the children of men, I sing.

It is swiftly and briefly developed, an enigmatic account of the
power of the "Almighty Father" with the news of "Sin and
Death destroyed". The main part of the brief work is concerned
with the prophecy to Manoa and the power of Samson as a
pure Nazarite. In the course of the poem the tragedy of Samson
is forgotten. But in a watercolour painted in about 1805 called
"Samson Subdued" the balance of the tragedy is achieved.
Here the powerful, muscular body appears wantonly feeble
and sapped of virtue.

It is well to maintain these comparisons over the centuries.
The original biblical version is a bare statement of violent
action with relatively little elaboration. The development of
this material in the hands of dramatist, poet, and painter over
several centuries of a growing tradition provides one of our
richest examples of the extended implications of source
material when it is handled by artists of insight.

7

Lord Byron: *Cain: A Mystery*

It was scarcely to be expected that in the highly rational period between Milton and the Romantic poets there should be any proliferation of religious drama. The theatre itself lived very considerably on the accumulated capital of the Jacobean age but treated its classical masterpieces with scant ceremony. The temper of the adaptations of Shakespeare, with the considerable exclusion of much of his sensitive examination of theological and moral problems, indicates the necessary modesty of our expectations about the religious significance of their original drama.

With the beginning of the Romantic period there was a break in the predominant rationalism. Metaphysical relationships could once more be explored in terms even of traditional theology, and the drama of the Romantic poets, though very derivative and dependent on Jacobean models, had a new intensity and moved into areas of speculation which had been largely absent in the literature since Shakespeare. Most of the major Romantic poets wrote plays, some of which had a qualified success in the theatre. Wordsworth's very clumsy *Borderers* plays a significant part in the development of his view of man and in particular of his doctrine of evil. Coleridge, and in the next generation Shelley, both contributed interesting if relatively uninfluential works to the dramatic consciousness of their age. There is, however, only one work during this period which merits close attention in the development of religious drama, Byron's *Cain*, which was published in 1821.

There is a pleasing effrontery of tone in Byron's preface; commenting on the "ancient title" of mystery which he has given the play, he claims to have kept nearer the scriptures than the authors of "those very profane productions", the medieval mysteries. He cites Warburton and Bishop Watson to support his readings of Genesis; he acknowledges the probable influence of Milton in the work but, conscious of precocity, he claims that "Gesner's 'Death of Abel' I have never read since I was eight years old".

Byron was always bitterly aware of the scandals which drove him from England; many of the central figures in his plays and long narrative poems are characteristic romantic rebels, asserting their own moral standards against society. In the body of Byron's work, then, *Cain* would seem to be ideally chosen as a final fling against social order; to take fratricide as a sympathetic subject would place Cain at the head of the "Byronic heroes". The tone of the preface appears to justify these expectations. He smiles at the traditional interpretations of Genesis: "If [Lucifer] disclaims having tempted Eve in the shape of a Serpent, it is only because the book of Genesis has not the most distant allusion to anything of the kind, but merely to the Serpent in his serpentine capacity." He is similarly ironic about the rôle which Lucifer is to play in his mystery: "With regard to the language of Lucifer, it was difficult to make him talk like a clergyman upon the same subjects; but I have done what I could to restrain him within the bounds of spiritual politeness." With this prefatory warning we anticipate almost any reversal of our moral expectations or of our usual scriptural readings.

In fact the tone of the play itself is very different. It opens, perhaps rather inflatedly, with the family prayers of Adam and his children, during which Cain alternates in mood between de-

fiance and apparent self-justification ("Abel, I'm sick at heart").
With the entry of Lucifer dramatic tension begins, which has to
sustain the long theological argument through the remainder
of Act I. In the course of this discussion, the tragedy of the third
act is anticipated in a fine irony of characterization. Cain cries
out to Lucifer:

> Thoughts unspeakable
> Crowd in my breast to burning, when I hear
> Of this almighty Death, who is, it seems
> Inevitable. Could I wrestle with him?

We have to wait until after Abel's murder for this irony to be
worked out:

> I—who abhor
> The name of Death so deeply, that the thought
> Empoison'd all my life, before I knew
> His aspect—I have led him here, and given
> My brother to his cold and chill embrace.

In Act II his sardonic tone returns; Lucifer, "prince of the
air", encourages Cain to fly through the "Abyss of Space" by a
demonic parody of St Peter's venture on the waves:

> There will come
> An hour, when, toss'd upon some water drops,
> A man shall say to a man, "Believe in me,
> And walk the waters", and the man shall walk.

They go beyond the living universe, traverse "Hades", while
Lucifer fallaciously undermines Cain's still powerful belief in
virtue and natural beauty. In Act III Cain returns to an almost
idyllic but restless interlude with Adah and his son Enoch,
which moves dramatically into the sacrifice of the two brothers.
Here Byron shows his greatest tact in craftsmanship. He has
understood the tension in the Old Testament between the
ideal of the shepherd and the cultivators of the Canaan plain

and he inverts these ideals in Cain; he makes his offering with
a conscious rejection of Abel's "blood sacrifice":

> I have no flocks;
> I am a tiller of the ground, and must
> Yield what it yieldeth to my toil—its fruit . . .
> If thou lov'st blood, the shepherd's shrine, which smokes
> On my right hand . . .
> If a shrine without a victim,
> An altar without gore, may win they favour,
> Look on it!

His sacrifice is rejected and in contempt of a God who demands
blood, he seeks to destroy the altar; in the struggle Abel is
killed, with the dying words:

> O God! receive thy servant and
> Forgive the slayer, for he knew not what
> He did.

(This tacit association of the death of Abel with the crucifixion
and with the martyrdom of St Stephen is an ancient one, found
in the Eucharist and the offices for St Stephen's day.)

The difficult passage after Abel's murder is the best handled
section of the play. In place of the rhetoric that might have
been feared, Zillah cries, after Cain's expression of horror:
"Father!—Eve!—Adah!—come hither! Death is in the world!"
to be followed by Cain's speech already quoted: "I—who abhor
the name of Death . . ." Indeed, Byron treats the central mystery of Cain's tragedy, the first awful entry of the unknown
state of death into the world, more powerfully than any of his
predecessors. This moment is followed by the futile curses of
Eve and the tenderness of Cain's wife, Adah, which prepares
for the dramatic strength of Cain's contrition. This begins with
Byron's significant modification of Cain's words as they are
found in the Genesis version: "Am I my brother's keeper?",
which becomes here: "Am I *then* my brother's keeper?"; the
single-word alteration brings bewilderment in place of

defiance; this begins his recognition that a relationship he had rejected was in fact valid. The angel's mark on his brow is welcomed for it is succeeded by self-knowledge and contrition:

> That which I am, I am; I did not seek
> For life, nor did I make myself; but could I
> With my own death redeem him from the dust—

The closing speeches bring Byron's play into line with the other versions to be considered below. The wilderness, the waste land, with the suggestion of the scapegoat wandering, is faced and even chosen as a way of purgation:

> Now for the wilderness
> Eastward from Eden will we take our way;
> 'Tis the most desolate, and suits my steps . . .

to which Adah's reply gives promise of reconciliation:

> Lead! thou shalt be my guide, and may our God
> Be thine! Now let us carry forth our children.

This then is a moving, exploratory play. There are some dull passages of Shavian argument, but the human and theological implications of the biblical narrative are never shirked, there is no sentimentalizing and no false justification of the "hero".

From this analysis it becomes possible to place Byron's play in the context of the tradition regarding Cain from the early liturgical drama through to the nineteenth century. It has already been hinted that the narrative in Genesis imposed certain intellectual strains on the story. Until we realize that the author of this section of the Genesis story is involved in the long tradition of conflict between the pastoral ideal and the tiller of the soil, the story of Cain and Abel appears to have an element of caprice. It is difficult to accept on the surface the motivation either for God's rejection of Cain's sacrifice or for Cain's aggressive rejection of Abel. When we realize however that sunk in the story is the fundamental assumption that the pastoral life (leading to its climax in the Davidic kingship, anticipating the shepherd rôle of Christ) is exemplified in the character of Abel, and the dangerous pagan religions of the fertile plains concentrated in the character of Cain, we lose the tensions which would be instinctive to the Jewish writer or reader. The absence of these assumptions in the explicit statement of the story accounts for the constant straining towards psychological explanation in the various dramatic treatments. This begins with the earliest of the treatments in the cycle plays.

The fifteenth-century *Killing of Abel* from the Wakefield cycle is a cruder play than the more familiar *Second Shepherds' Play* from the same group. It is given local actuality by the contrast between the God-fearing, tithe-giving Abel and the vigorously foul-mouthed ploughman, Cain. There is a grotesque humour in the greed with which Cain tells up his sheaves, selecting the smallest and mustiest for sacrifice; but the tragedy is huddled into some sixteen lines, with the unprepared transition from Cain's rough jest to the slain Abel:

> So, lig down ther and take thi rest . . .

to his stricken address to the audience almost at once:

> Bot now, syn he is broght on slepe,
> Into som hole fayn wold I crepe.

The seventeenth century intensified the significance of this tragically oblique reference to death in "broght on slepe". Henry Vaughan, with characteristic insight, in his poem "Death" emphasizes the tragic mystery that this is the first entrance of death into the created order:

> Though since thy first sad entrance by
> Just *Abel's* death,

an important element in the theological interpretation of the Genesis mythology.

Milton treats the theme briefly in *Paradise Lost*, Book XI, lines 556–636. It is difficult to isolate this short passage from the argument of the whole poem, but it is certainly an unexpected interpretation of Cain. At the opening of Book I the consequences of sin are clearly stated:

> Of Mans First Disobedience, and the Fruit
> Of that Forbidden Tree, whose mortal tast
> Brought Death into the World.

Yet Cain, the instrument of death, is barely mentioned in the eleventh book; he is simply the "one who slew his Brother". Instead of considering Cain, his offspring are described as sophisticated worldlings:

> Studious they appere
> Of Arts that polish Life, inventors rare,
> Unmindful of thir Maker.

At length their sophistication turns to "effeminate slackness" and they fall through lechery, a principal and abiding theme in Milton, but an importation to the Cain story, though it links Cain with the luxury and sin associated throughout the Old Testament with the "cities of the plain" where his progeny dwelt.

The more numerous developments of the Cain theme in the Romantic period are anticipated and largely influenced by Salomon Gessler's prose romance, *Der Tod Abels*, published in 1758 (I quote from the English translation published in 1816). A good deal of its interest lies in Adam's recapitulation of the Fall—there is a vivid biblical echo in his description of the dawn of human fear: "I secured the entrance of the grotto with entwined brambles." The death-theme is not yet completely realized as it was to be in Byron, but there is an interesting motivation for the murder in the inversion of the pastoral theme. Cain dreams the fate of his offspring: "He saw his sons bound, and with their wives and infants, tamely marching before the children of Abel, like a flock of bleating sheep." But these insights are not maintained and after the murder of Abel the tale declines into excessive posturing and lamentation.

Gessler closed his story with the departure of Cain into the desert regions, "where had never been imprinted the foot of man". This was the main motive of the Romantic treatment of Cain, notably in Coleridge's strangely neglected *Wanderings of Cain*, written probably in 1797–8. This has an especially fine rendering of the landscape of dereliction into which Cain flees:

> The scene around was desolate; as far as the eye could reach it was desolate: the bare rocks faced each other, and left a long and wide interval of thin white sand . . . The pointed and shattered summits of the ridges of the rocks made a rude mimicry of human concerns and seemed to prophesy mutely of things that then were not; steeples, and battlements, and ships with naked masts.

This is Coleridge's Waste Land, as *The Ancient Mariner* is his Waste Sea, and Cain fittingly matches the Mariner in dereliction.

Blake's *The Ghost of Abel* (engraved in 1822), an examination of the theme which is extended by his poignant drawing, "Abel found by Adam and Eve", is explicitly a reply "To Lord Byron in the Wilderness"; it takes yet another line of interpretation. Abel is a spirit crying for vengeance, for, wandering in the shades, he cannot forgive:

> My soul in fumes of blood
> Cries for Vengeance, Sacrifice on Sacrifice, Blood on Blood!

to which Jehovah gives the final conclusion of the Cain myth:

> Lo! I have given you a Lamb for an Atonement, instead
> Of the Transgressor, or no Flesh or Spirit could ever live.

With this assurance the Ghost of Abel is stilled and Satan defeated.

The Cain narrative then is complex and far-reaching. From Genesis to Byron and Blake, the association of sin, death, sacrifice, and atonement transfigure the violent primitive theme of fratricide.

8

Lord Tennyson: *Becket*

The moral pressure put upon man's loyalty by the claims of secular and sacred activities have rarely been more precisely focused than in the career of Thomas Becket. It is not for nothing that in our own day, when moral choices in the public sphere are rarely between clear right and wrong but more frequently between varying degrees of duty, the career of St Thomas of Canterbury should have become as central a symbol of this choice as Antigone has been in the sphere of personal moral choice. The dual career of Chancellor and Archbishop, united in one man and setting up immediate and apparently insoluble tensions, has struck three dramatists of our own day as of profoundly contemporary importance; it is perhaps rather more surprising that Tennyson should have found, in the more urbane political climate of the Victorian era, that this was a significant theme for his major historical play. As we shall see, Tennyson's *Becket* has few of the tensions compassed by Eliot and Fry and indeed moves into a more personal sphere of reference than either *Murder in the Cathedral* or *Curtmantle*, but the fundamental problem remains in Tennyson the problem which has made Thomas Becket a central figure in our legal and ecclesiastical history.

When Browning published *Strafford* in 1837, he dedicated it—on 23 April—"In all affectionate admiration to William C.

Macready", one of the finest Shakespearean actors of his day.
Nearly a half-century later, in 1884, Tennyson published *Becket*,
dedicating it with historical propriety, not to an actor but to a
statesman, Lord Selborne: "To you, the honoured Chancellor
of our own day, I dedicate this dramatic memorial of your
great predecessor;—which, altho' not intended in its present
form to meet the exigencies of our modern theatre, has nevertheless . . . won your approbation." In spite of Tennyson's disclaimer in this dedication, Henry Irving found *Becket* splendidly
suited to his craft, and he adapted and produced it in 1893.

These two poets, Tennyson and Browning, illustrate the
dilemma of the dramatist in an age when poetry is not a
spontaneous language for the theatre. For over two centuries
after the death of Shakespeare, poetry held an equivocal position in drama. The first twenty years of the seventeenth century
saw the final shaping of verse as an instrument of dramatic expression, and saw also its supple relation with prose within the
same plays. No ready formula describes this joint function:
Marlowe could on occasion be seen struggling with a recalcitrant instrument of expression; much of his creative effort
went into shaping it, but no such struggle is seen in Shakespeare. His technique changed and matured but this was an
organic development and not against the collar. Briefly: earlier
drama had few resources to express certain relationships, attitudes, problems; no such merely technical difficulty existed
for Shakespeare, Jonson, or Webster.

With the closing of the theatres, an age in dramatic development ended. The Restoration had other matters of concern,
the theatre was at once more complex and less subtle, and
dramatic language had changed in its forms of suppleness. The
eighteenth century saw no great tragedy and the Comedy of
Manners declined into Sheridan. Romantic and post-Romantic
poets, then, had no tradition of poetic drama to sustain them;
frequently (and this was the dilemma of Wordsworth and

Coleridge) blank verse was adopted in an attempt to bridge the gap with the Jacobean age, its discontinuity with the verse of the Shakespearean theatre being the more apparent by the Romantics' constraint in handling the line.

In these circumstances, the flexibility of Tennyson's treatment in *Becket* is the more surprising. The cast of the play is almost prodigal in numbers, designed to emphasize contrast in theme and motive: Henry is set against Becket, the group of bishops and archbishops balance the knights, Brito, Fitzurse, Tracy, and Morville: most piquant of the contrasts, Queen Eleanor of Aquitaine overshadows in depth and range of character the fair Rosamund, who might be assumed to be a natural romantic heroine. Eleanor as queen and wife, skilled in the courts of love and the arts of diplomacy, vies with Becket as Tennyson's most interesting dramatic creation.

The theme also is handled without the naïvety which mars earlier romantic drama. The clash between Henry and Becket, which is neither deeply motivated nor raised to any great emotional tension, is nevertheless understood at personal, legal, and ecclesiastical levels. These may be seen more clearly in examining the plot, the structure of which is a little too obtrusive.

The prologue efficiently sets the main theme of the play through the ambiguities of the chess game between Henry and Becket:

HENRY
By the royal customs of our realm
The Church should hold her baronies of me,
Like other lords amenable to law.

BECKET
My liege, I move my bishop.

HENRY   And if I live,
No man without my leave shall excommunicate
My tennants or my household.

BECKET
Look to your king . . .
                    You see my bishop
Hath brought your king to a standstill.

When the romance theme of Rosamund, the royal paramour, has been introduced, Eleanor's character is firmly established, ironic, suave, with an unexpected tenderness in the songs which might have been from *The Princess*:

Over and gone with the roses
Not over and gone with the rose.

By comparison with the complexity of Eleanor, Rosamund is a curiously lay figure.

The central scene in the first part of the play is the powerful conflict in the "Hall of Northampton Castle" (I. iii). The important feature in the setting is the very Elizabethan "chair royal" which focuses the conflict for power, with the ecclesiastical synod surrounded by the watchful group of knights. Tennyson realizes the scene with a deft feeling for subordinate climaxes—Becket's signing but refusing to seal the concordat with the throne and finally protecting himself beneath the processional cross. It was fine stage stuff for Irving.

The following scene (I. iv), appears to show the direct influence of Shakespeare's early Histories. The poor man, the dog, the three beggars, the four knights, are employed with a consciously "symbolic" intention, but the scene, effective enough within its own bounds, pulls against the prevailing tone and manner of the Act and against the lyrical romanticism of Act II, in Rosamund's Bower. The whole opening movement of the play demonstrates the flaccid structure inevitable when poetry in "poetic drama" is a decorative addition or even a device added to heighten intellectual content or emotional pressure. It is illuminating to break off reading at this point to contrast the terse economy with which Eliot develops an analogous theme and the same historical material in *Murder in the Cathedral*.

The last three acts are notable for the successive development of character. The return to Rosamund's Bower in Act III provides one of the unexpected pleasures of the play in the character of Margery. Her entry, when we have already heard her singing off-stage, is admirable:

> Babble in bower
> Under the rose!
> Bee mustn't buzz,
> Whoops—but he knows.

I ha' been but a week here but I ha' seen what I ha' seen . .

The long soliloquy which follows appears to be a nice variant on Juliet's nurse, and even if no more than a parody, would have its pleasant ironies. But the song places her more firmly in Tennyson's own poetic world, the people of his own (and too little valued) dialect poetry.

Act IV carries further the direct struggle between Eleanor and Rosamund, hovering uneasily between the novelettish and true dramatic conflict. Although Rosamund is in effect the ward of Becket, the "love theme" in the play is never fully integrated with the motives of the main plot.

With the fifth act the movement becomes terser and more effective (as it squares more accurately with chronicle history). At Becket's determination: "Undo the door: the church is not a castle" (compare the dramatic moment in Eliot's handling of this scene, beginning "Unbar the door"), the climax of martyrdom comes swiftly. The speeches alternate, without too much strain, between natural dialogue and a stylistic formality to which liturgical and scriptural echoes give strength:

Storm bursts

MORVILLE
Will the earth gape and swallow us alive?

*Flashes of lightning thro' the Cathedral. Rosamund seen
kneeling by the body of Becket.*

Indeed, though we have none of the subtle probing of motive
which makes the figure of Eliot's Becket so notable, the tension
of martyrdom, of personal sin and the deviousness of statecraft, raise the closing act to the highest point in the play and
to a remarkable achievement in an age devoid of original tragic
writing and wholly dependent on its qualified reverence for
Shakespeare to maintain its hold on poetic expression in the
theatre.

Tennyson had tacitly set himself two problems: to write a
poetic play which should nevertheless be not unsuitable for the
theatre (in spite of the preface disclaimer) and to cope with the
always recalcitrant chronicle form. The one we have seen to
have been at least fairly successful; the second, the handling
of time within the chronicle sequence, was more trouble-
some.

The Greek dramatic form, developing the significances of a
critical moment in the fortunes of the characters, had by-
passed the question which preoccupied the Elizabethans,
namely, the slow ordering of fortune by the actions of providence. Whether this is seen as the controlling hand of a personal God or as blind movement in destiny, time is required in
its working out. When this preoccupation was reinforced for
the Elizabethans by a growing sense of history as the "secular"
expression of providence, the way was clear for the transformation of the chronicle play into historical tragedy, as we see it
growing, from Gorboduc, through Marlowe's *Edward II*,
Shakespeare's *Henry VI* and *Richard III*, to the mature History
plays, English and Roman.

The Romantic revival of history had no such profound

springs. Antiquarian interest in a colourful past, picturesque setting and costume, overshadowed any real attempt in the theatre to interpret history creatively.

Tennyson's success and failure are both interesting and did not suffer disastrously, as we shall see in two later chapers, by comparison with the treatment by Eliot and Fry. The material in *Becket* is handled chronologically. He fails to transform the pedestrian chronicle through isolating the development of a significant theme. Yet for Tennyson there is a compensating success: the spiritual conflict of Becket, divided between his loyalty to Henry, his duty to Eleanor, and—by an extension of sanctuary—to Rosamund, is genuinely if not deeply perceived. It is no negligible moment in the Victorian contribution to religious themes in the theatre.

9

T. S. Eliot: *Family Reunion*

T. S. Eliot's concern with the substance and the technique of drama has coincided with the whole of his critical career and for half that time he has been actively concerned with writing drama. Two of his works *The Rock* and *Murder in the Cathedral* have been quite explicitly religious drama; none of his dramatic works has been without specific relation to moral, social, and theological problems. Indeed one of the critical adventures in the reading of Eliot's work has been to follow the skill with which theological preoccupations have in many ways intensified while becoming more and more oblique in their statement.

As critic T. S. Eliot has been able to achieve a quite extraordinary objectivity concerning his own work. Some of his most important criticism of poetry has been an implicit and frequently an explicit examination of the revolution in poetic practice in which he was a major participant. In relation to his dramatic work, rarely can any poet or playwright have given such a coolly objective survey of his own development as we had from Eliot in *Poetry and Drama* (1951), in which success and failure were recorded with a clinical impartiality which would have seemed enviable if the critic had been handling the work of a writer of a past generation; it was a moving piece of creative humility, when we realize that the subject of criticism was Eliot's own work.

In the last chapter we found in Tennyson's *Becket* a characteristic example of "closet drama" dependent upon a pedestrian imitation of Elizabethan blank verse. Eliot has been a leading interpreter of Elizabethan drama, and because of his understanding of its verse in the theatre, he has himself been in no danger of a reverential return to blank verse as the inevitable medium for poetic statement of the stage. The movement of speech is never absent from his non-dramatic verse, from the *Preludes* to the *Quartets*, and in the transition piece, *Sweeney Agonistes*, we find the spasmodic simplified syntax of half-formulated conversational language, which he describes in *Poetry and Drama* as a medium distinguished from formulated prose. The opening of *Sweeney* is established upon a firm rhythmic beat but across it there is syncopated the tentative and broken rhythms of conversation, the half repetitions which formulate the meaning by a series of exploratory advances and retreats, a method which anticipates Harold Pinter's technique for expressing inarticulateness in dramatic language.

> DORIS
> I like Sam
>
> DUSTY   *I* like Sam
> Yes and Sam's a nice boy too.
> He's a funny fellow
>
> DORIS   He *is* a funny fellow
> He's like a fellow once I knew.
> *He* could make you laugh.
>
> DUSTY   Sam can make you laugh:
> Sam's all right
>
> DORIS   But Pereira won't do.

Probably the most remarkable feat in *Sweeney* is to anticipate, in the vulgar little melodrama the later, profound preoccupation with the imprecision and decline in meaning of the words we use, the "raid on the inarticulate". In Sweeney's attempt to explain the meaningless monotony of existence to Doris and

Dusty, one passage closely anticipates the fifth movement of *Burnt Norton*. Sweeney is impatient with words as an instrument of communication.

> Death or life or life or death
> Death is life and life is death
> *I gotta use words* when I talk to you
> But if you understand or if you don't
> That's nothing to me and nothing to you
> We all gotta do what we gotta do.

With more elegance the idea is extended in *Burnt Norton*.

> Words strain,
> Crack and sometimes break, under the burden,
> Under the tension, slip, slide, perish,
> Decay with imprecision, will not stay in place,
> Will not stay still.

In some respects *Sweeney Agonistes* is a more mature fulfilment of Eliot's ideal of the language of theatre than the next play, *The Rock*; but in the latter play, essentially an "occasional piece" written to assist a fund for building churches, he first shaped in English the instrument of the Chorus which he used most maturely in *Murder in the Cathedral* and probably less effectually in *Family Reunion*. It is significant that the Choruses from *The Rock* are all that he has now allowed to remain in print. In their union of the liturgical beat of scriptural language with the brooding exploratoriness of his non-dramatic work, these, with the Choruses from *Murder in the Cathedral*, demonstrate the degree of success which we can hope from choric speech in the theatre and, as Eliot argued in *Poetry and Drama*, almost certainly demonstrate its inappropriateness in our age. Certainly in the hands of anyone less skilled than Eliot the choric ode can lead to disastrous preciosity.

Yeats and Eliot were faced with a situation in which poetry in the theatre was a literary "problem". Was it a flight from the realism in which dramatic themes, the themes of Ibsen,

Shaw, and Galsworthy, were to be expressed? These questions have been debated by theorists and still preoccupy critics. Yet to Eliot verse has never been problematical as a form of dramatic expression. The sole "problem" has been the degree of intensity, allusiveness, and concentration which could be assimilated by an audience at any passing moment in the theatre. Eliot therefore rejects the easy distinction between the prose play of realism and the verse play of exaltation and fantasy. For him, as a writer in the theatre, a full spectrum of techniques is open: from the broken half-formulations of "conversation", through the sophisticated rhythms of "prose", to the modest intensity of "verse" and ultimately to the exaltation and high intensity of dramatic poetry. Unlike the particularity of prose then, verse could allow the dramatic writer more elbow-room. At certain points in the action it will scarcely be recognized as "poetic" (this low pitch of intensity, where the technique has been pared away to a point where the poetry is barely defined from prose, was Eliot's avowed aim in the greater part of *The Confidential Clerk*); but where the dramatic conflict permitted it verse could assume a complexity and universality impossible to prose:

> It will only be poetry when the dramatic situation has reached such a point of intensity that poetry becomes the natural dramatic utterance, because then it is the only language in which the emotions can be expressed at all.

This conscious direction of his technique, deliberate manipulation of the dramatic instrument, has been the special achievement of a writer who has always been poet and critic, never dissociating analysis from creative writing.

For a Christian poet and dramatist such as Eliot, history has a particular, providential significance. History in the theatre can never maintain a mere archaeological interest, a remote aesthetic charm, like a tourist's affection for a cathedral. The past is of course always more than contemporary—there is no confounding of historical sequence in a formless lump—but the past has never less than a contemporary relevance, and the present loses any triviality it might possess through a constant reinterpretation in terms of past events.

Eliot has achieved this dual perspective of past and present by two related means. In *Murder in the Cathedral* past events, realized with historical integrity within the reign of Henry II, are sharply reorientated in terms of our own age through the colloquial idiom of the four knights; we are addressed directly in the prose terms of our own day. It adds something to our understanding of Becket's significance in the contemporary world when he is commended by one of the knights for having the competence to reach the highest ranks of the Civil Service; ironic anachronism is a valuable instrument in the hands of the historical dramatist. In the three plays after *Murder* the technique is reversed; the theme and setting are contemporary, the language, though poetry, is in our vocabulary and idiom. But the historical perspective is achieved by the underlying reference to classical tragedy, comedy, or myth; in *Family Reunion* the reference is tragic, to the *Oresteia*. The French theatre of Sartre, Giraudoux, and Anouilh has employed the same means to distance and objectify modern dilemmas.

Despite the concentration which Eliot achieves by the strict limitation of the theme in *Murder in the Cathedral* and the illusion of uniformity which the consistent dignity of the verse forms appears to give the play, there is a remarkable range of technique shown, when we compare the first three plays of Eliot's dramatic output. Even *Murder* itself exhibits the flexibility of range from the most intense choric odes at the beginning and end of the second act to the direct and deliberately clumsy wit of the prose used by the four knights. Even at the moments of highest tragic intensity Eliot allows a tone of half-ironic detachment to point the tragedy. The peremptory authority of Becket's command to the fearful monks, "Unbar the door" is mitigated by the complex tones of his declaration, "I am not in any danger, only near to death".

Nevertheless despite the mastery of this technical range Eliot felt that a new departure had to be undertaken in his statement of themes in the theatre. In *The Rock* and *Murder* he was sharing a common language with a body of Christian people who were a minority within the theatre-going public. These were plays explicitly in the form of religious drama; *Murder in the Cathedral* was written to commission for the Canterbury Festival, deriving on its first presentation a further strong emotional impulse from the coincidence of its setting with the historical tragedy of Becket. Eliot's determination, which he explains in *Poetry and Drama*, was now to extend these explorations of moral and religious themes into the setting of the commercial theatre. What had formerly been done in terms of church and cathedral had now to become valid in the atmosphere and in the tones and vocabulary of Shaftesbury Avenue. This necessarily involves both a limitation and an extension of the range of his dramatic technique. There is a limitation in so far as he can no longer count on a shared vocabulary as an expression of shared beliefs and religious assumptions. There is an extension in that these assumptions and beliefs have now to be stated with a newly formulated rhetoric and persuasion to people who do not share them. The explicit and the formulated has now to become the oblique and the persuasive. This complex task is first attempted in *Family Reunion*.

One brief passage in the first scene of the play demonstrates the flexibility of the verse form which T. S. Eliot has at his disposal. Harry, Lord Monchensey, is confronted at Wishwood by his two blunt-minded uncles, Gerald and Charles:

HARRY
People to whom nothing has ever happened
Cannot understand the unimportance of events.

GERALD
Well you can't say that nothing has happened to *me*.
I started as a youngster on the North-West Frontier—
Been in tight corners most of my life
And in some pretty nasty messes.

CHARLES
And there isn't much would surprise me,
Or shock me, either.

HARRY   You are all people
To whom nothing has happened, at most a continual impact
Of external events. You have gone through life in sleep,
Never woken to the nightmare. I tell you, life would be un-
  endurable
If you were wide awake.

Here the characters are clearly differentiated by the three
rhythms, the brooding contemplative length of Harry's lines,
the staccato pseudo-crispness of the army officer, the nudging
bonhomie of the clubman. Through the intensity of verse or
through its complete abandonment, Eliot can achieve the contrasts between the deliberate witty banality of a police-court
report:

> While trying to extricate his car from the collision, Mr. Piper re-
> versed into a shop-window. When challenged, Mr. Piper said, "I
> thought it was all open country about here" [in Ebury Street].

and the mounting exaltation of Agatha's speech to Harry:

What we have written is not a story of detection,
Of crime and punishment, but of sin and expiation.
                    You may learn hereafter,
Moving alone through flames of ice, chosen
To resolve the enchantment under which we suffer.

The flexibility and range of the verse forms in this play then
enabled Eliot to move with comparative ease between many
levels of reference in his plot and his characterization. At one

level it could, like the plays which have succeeded *Family Reunion*, be interpreted as a direct human story of the tragedies and tensions inside a family. At this level it is a grave examination of those mental and emotional depths which had been necessarily neglected by the domestic comedies of the previous quarter century. But at another level it reaches the intensity of almost universal myth. The retention of verse enabled Eliot also to retain from his classical model two elements in his plot of which in fact he has elsewhere expressed doubts: the pursuing Eumenides, menacing Harry with the individual and corporate guilt of his family; and the Chorus whose personal identities become subordinate to the formal verse movement. This latter is conspicuously so in the conclusion of the play in which the members of the family unite in a formal, almost liturgical movement which has overtones of both Christian chant and of magic.

> This way the pilgrimage
> Of expiation
> Round and round the circle
> Completing the charm
> So the knot be unknotted
> The crossed be uncrossed
> The crooked be made straight
> And the curse be ended.

The other element retained, the pursuing fates (who were so awkwardly unmanageable in the conditions of the theatre) nevertheless, particularly in a reading of the play, provide an important link between pre-Christian and Christian elements in this present study of ours. Eliot is by no means the only dramatist to have exploited the powerful intellectual and emotional qualities of our theological inheritance from the Greeks. We owe no insignificant debt to classical civilization for providing us with much of the vocabulary and the categories for exploring man's mind which has now achieved the status of a science in the presuppositions of psychoanalysis. This in turn has been drawn upon by our contemporary writers so that the wheel has come full circle: a Greek dramatist explores the tragedy of Oedipus; his tragedy provides a focal point for the psychoanalyst's examination of the Oedipus complex; this understanding of unconscious impulse and overwhelming sense of guilt becomes the raw material of a writer's craft. So with Eliot's use of Greek prototypes. The image of Orestes and the objectified guilt by which he is pursued stimulates the examination of family relationships in modern society. The deliberate ambiguity by which we are left in doubt whether or not Harry was formally guilty of the death of his wife, reinforces the tragic fact that there are obscure currents in human relationships which have far greater tragic consequences than formal stories of "detection, of crime and punishment". All this is implied and to a limited extent successfully mediated by Eliot's adoption of a convention of pursuing Eumenides from his Greek original.

There is a very complex subtlety in Eliot's handling of character in this play. As a play it declares itself to be the tragedy of a family; it is a story of "sin and expiation", and though the explicitly Christian terms are infrequent—though strongly present in the word "sin" itself, in the ice and flame of purgation, and in the charity which moves through the relations of Harry with Mary and Agatha—the Christian themes are insistent. This is clearly a handling of sin, of the burden of guilt and ultimate redemption, which is in part vicarious. One of the dramatic means by which this theme has been objectified is the differentiation between the lay-figures of the family and the fully realized, compassionate figures of Agatha, Mary, and Harry himself. Amy, Violet, Gerald, and Charles are never merely puppets, but their blunt incomprehension of the tragedy worked out in their presence deprives them of the fullest human stature. In these three lines the characters of Violet and Gerald are fully differentiated, etched in Amy's irony:

> Gerald, you are the stupidest person in this room,
> Violet, you are the most malicious in a harmless way;
> I prefer your company to that of any of the others.

This is the tone which provides the foil to the explorations which make the relations between Harry and Agatha among the profoundest moments on our contemporary stage.

10

Christopher Fry

Critical caprice, both among theatre critics and scholars, has made it difficult to make a just appraisal of Christopher Fry's work as a dramatist, and as a religious dramatist in particular. Among those who are "professionally" engaged in religious drama, he has been consistently esteemed and performed; his output has been punctuated by plays readily set in this genre: *The Boy with a Cart*, *The Firstborn*, *Thor with Angels*, and *A Sleep of Prisoners*. But critical controversy has centred upon the plays that are not obviously in the area of liturgy or dogma. *A Phoenix too Frequent* and *The Lady's Not for Burning* were assumed to have established the Fry manner and tone, with, as one critic put it wholly misleadingly, "an Elizabethan splendour of phrase". An immediate result of the critical excitement over these two plays (accentuated by the drabness of the war years, making this verbal scintillation the more welcome) was a sense of surprise and even frustration at the wholly different quality of *The Dark is Light Enough* and *Curtmantle*. Proper assessment can be reached only by recognizing first the amazing versatility of Fry's talent and, even more important, its consistency and unity.

For thirty years Christopher Fry has been engaged in a variety of media, from the grace of his collaboration in *She Shall have Music* in 1935 to the grave explorations of *Curtmantle* in 1962. During these years he has composed music for the Herbert

Wilcox film of *The Beggar's Opera* and for Peter Brook's production of *The Winter's Tale*; throughout this time he has
written lyric poetry; he has written for radio and television and
for the cinema, in William Wyler's *Ben Hur* and Richard
Fleischer's *Barabbas*. He has been the dramatist most successful
in naturalizing the French theatre in England with his translations of Anouilh and Giraudoux, while in lectures and articles
he has maintained a consistent critical appraisal of contemporary dramatic theory.

Versatility in the arts is a quality of which we have always
been deeply suspicious, demanding that the creative artist—in
denial of the Renaissance ideal—concern himself with few
media, limited themes and images, working with intensity
within a narrow range. A writer as varied as Christopher Fry
could perhaps have avoided adverse criticism of some aspects
of his work by some such distinction, as Anouilh's, between his
pièces roses and *pièces noires* or that of Graham Greene between
his novels and his "entertainments". In fact any such distinction would have been at least as false in Fry's work as it tends
to be in Anouilh's or Greene's. On any serious analysis the most
impressive fact in Fry's work is its integrity and homogeneity;
against the popular assumption that his "typical" work is
effervescent or flippant, the marks allegedly characterizing
The Lady's Not for Burning and *A Phoenix too Frequent*, we have
the constant recurrence of tragedy as his dominant mode, in
The Firstborn, *The Dark is Light Enough*, and *Curtmantle*, and in
the festival play *Thor with Angels*; this consistently recurring
gravity contrasts with the variety of tone in his comedies: the
gentle near-homiletic quality of *The Boy with a Cart*; the witty,
mythical allusiveness of *A Phoenix*; the other gravity—which
requires closer examination—of *The Lady's Not for Burning*; the
mature disenchantment of *Venus Observed*; each of these works
implies a new approach to comedy and each of them has undertones of argument which trespass on the theological. *A*

Sleep of Prisoners rejects any regular classification. Commissioned quite specifically for the 1951 Festival by the Religious Drama Society of Great Britain it explores the theme of sacrifice and expiation in a series of dreaming and working states, recreating the tragic dilemmas of Adam, Cain, Abraham, David, all those "figures of wisdom back in the old sorrows", from creation, through the Three Children in the fiery furnace, to the crucifixion of Christ. Yet this exploration of "what makes for life and what makes for death" (Fry's summary of the theme in his dedication to Robert Gittings) has a delicacy and wit, sometimes trespassing on levity, which deny its sombre nature. The philosophy behind this essential unity of tragedy and comedy may be found in a recent note by Fry which comments on Teilhard de Chardin's "organic crisis in [moral] evolution". Christopher Fry writes:

> We know that the way we mature is through a series of crises, of one sort or another. We reach an obstacle, and learn to overcome it; our thoughts or emotions become knotted, and we increase ourselves in order to unknot them; a state of being becomes intolerable, and, drawing upon a hidden reserve of spirit, we transform it. There comes, as it were, a tension of imprisonment before the vigour which sets us free; a sensation of death, before the rebirth.

The play of most unrelieved tragic intensity is *The Firstborn*; published in 1948, there had been a ten-year gap in its writing (a period which spanned the war) and this interval had bitten deep into Fry's dramatic craft. This can be seen very clearly if this play is compared with *The Boy with a Cart*, which, with all its personal grace, was strongly under the rhythmic influence and the tone of voice of Eliot. *The Firstborn* is dark throughout; the tragic conflict moves in two parallel tensions, the violence of God's plagues upon Egypt, with Moses as their instrument, and the internal conflict of personality, Moses against Seti. This is clear enough in dramatic structure; but Fry has recognized

26570

an unspoken, latent tragedy in the biblical story, which intensifies the emotional tone of the play, namely that Moses, as an adopted Egyptian princeling, was brought up with Seti; that intimate boyhood, observed in our reading of the Old Testament chronology, consciously focuses the tragic violence of the play.

Thor with Angels was written for the 1948 Canterbury Festival and remains the most uncomplex of Fry's mature plays. It adopts the northern myth of crucifixion and conflates it with Christian history, using this dual sacrifical image to explore the dogmatic dilemma that broods over all Fry's work: the nature of suffering and sacrifice and above all their *necessity*. In *Thor* it is partially resolved in the near-dogmatic statement of Cymen towards the end of the play:

> For sacrifice
> Can only perfectly be made by God,
> And sacrifice has been made, by God
> To God in the body of God with man.

But in fact such an intellectual resolution in direct statement is rare in Fry's very exploratory, undogmatic work. A moment of essentially dramatic quality approaches a solution more sensitively in this play. Hoel is to be killed:

> Bring him to the tree; we'll offer him
> In Woden's way, the Woden death.

In the succeeding lines, Martina's cry to her human father is joined to a direct invocation of God by Hoel, the two simple speeches united in a dramatic trinitarian statement:

> MARTINA
> Father! Father!
>
> HOEL   Son and the brooding dove.
> Call him again.

These are the moments, when creed is crystallized into dramatic speech, that give specifically religious drama its validity.

In many respects *The Lady's Not for Burning* is Christopher Fry's greatest liability, obscuring by its witty success both its own greater qualities and the profounder plays which followed. By 1949 drab austerities without the impetus of war made audiences more than ready for a play in which (according to *The New Statesman* review of the first production) "we are launched into a sea of dazzling verbal invention which never for a moment flags". Among those works intended by Fry to celebrate the seasons this is a spring play, of "light, inconstant April sunshine, sunset, twilight and full-moon", but within this fresh gaiety critics have failed to notice the gravity behind the rather deprecating foreword. There he wrote that the play is concerned with "human intelligences in a dance together, sometimes with nothing but buoyancy, sometimes with a seriousness which has been sufficiently mocked by distress to be able to mock back". The impression in the first Gielgud, Pamela Brown, Richard Burton performance was certainly more of gaiety than of tragedy overcome, and it would be critically pretentious to speak of Thomas Mendip's "death wish" and its transcendence in charity—the play does not operate in this mode of argument. But when Jennet Jourdemayne, persecuted as a witch, makes her affirmation of the fundamental rationality of the natural order, the graver tones of the play must be attended to. Jennet's central opposition to the irrationality of those who hunt her as a witch is perfectly clear:

> I am Jennet Jourdemayne
> And I believe in the human mind . . .
>   What, does everyone still knuckle
> And suckle at the big breast of irrational fears?
> Do they really think I charm a sweat from Tagus . .
> Can they think and then think like this?

The light grace of her argument tightens into greater precision

at the end of the first act and we get a first hint of Fry's concern
with the inter-related lines of the universe:

> May I, Jennet Jourdemayne, the daughter
> Of a man who believed the universe was governed
> By certain laws, be allowed to speak?
> Here is such a storm of superstition
> And humbug and curious passions, where will you start
> To look for the truth.

Those certain, predictable laws which Jennet derived from her
father's speculations frequently function in the plays as a witty
pattern of "cosmic imagery"; more recently an intellectual
feeling for a kind of "emergent evolution" has taken more precise shape, partly under the influence of Teilhard de Chardin's
works, perhaps more powerfully from the needs of the legal
and historical arguments which led to his writing *Curtmantle*.
Some of the moments of greatest agony in *The Firstborn* came
from doubting the providential rationality of things; despite
the clarity with which retribution in the form of plagues appeared to follow inevitably upon the sins of Egypt, Aaron's
agony significantly takes the form of doubt, an inversion of
Jennet's affirmation:

> I've begun to believe that the reasonable
> Is an invention of man, altogether in opposition
> To the facts of creation.

But the more usual mode, even in the sombre *Firstborn*, is of
affirmation, a conviction that the will of God "made the crucial
interchange of earth with everlasting", that "even Dust can
speak, as it does in Moses now". But the maturity of this process has to wait for *Curtmantle*. Here a central tragic irony
points the whole process of thought of which this play is the
culmination: that Henry II works for due process of law which
is ultimately an expression of God's order, and that Becket,
subdued to God's will which is precisely the law towards
which Henry's ambitions are directed, finds himself in personal

opposition to Henry. The protagonists are in tragic conflict,
seemingly directed towards conflicting ends, while, since each
is in part instrumental, not wholly seeing the ends they serve,
they fail to see those areas in which the orders of positive law
and God's will overlap. In the conflict in the first act between
Becket and Henry there is a momentary return to an image
familiar to us from earlier plays:

> It's the nature of man that argues;
> The deep roots of disputation
> Which dug in the dust, and formed Adam's body.

But this play has gone beyond these earlier expressions and
Fry has hitherto given no profounder statement of the exploratory ends of his drama than in Becket's clear perception
of the opposition between himself and Henry. The clarity of
Henry's mind assumes that the device of uniting archbishop
and chancellor in one man resolves the dispute of divine and
secular law; Becket more fully realizes the essential instru-
mentality of man's will, as, at its highest form, wholly sub-
missive to the way of providence:

> You're dividing us, and, what is more, forcing
> Yourself and me, indeed the whole kingdom,
> Into a kind of intrusion on the human mystery,
> Where we may not know what it is we're doing,
> What powers we are serving, or what is being made of us,
> Or even understand the conclusion when it comes.
> Delivering us up, in fact, to universal workings
> Which neither you nor I wish to comply with
> Or even to contemplate.

This is a dramatic mode which goes far beyond any conven-
tional dogmatic demand of "religious drama" and which
makes *Curtmantle* one of the two or three finest plays of our
generation.

Meanwhile, in 1954, Fry had published *The Dark is Light
Enough*, produced at the Aldwych Theatre with Dame Edith
Evans in the same year. This was an important play in

Christopher Fry's development. After the critical acclaim for *A Phoenix too Frequent* and *The Lady's Not for Burning* (and the highly specialized technique of *A Sleep of Prisoners*) this was the first play to take a manifestly serious theme with complete gravity of tone. The theme was highly-charged emotionally, particularly in the years that followed the war, in handling the tragic tensions of marriage across racial boundaries, and the complementary themes of compassion, integrity, and the tentative growth of human relationships. All these were to be explored by Fry with hints of the old wit,

> (She bowed to us in the doorway, and said
> "We must freely admit the future", and withdrew
> To give birth to Stefan),

but the tone of the verse had on the whole become more sombre—confounding the critics, for whom *The Lady* and *A Phoenix* had become the norm.

The play has a simple structure, set in a *salon* presided over by a gracious and witty goddess:

> Why do you think I blaspheme?
> You know the Countess has the qualities of true divinity,
> For instance, how apparently undemandingly
> She moves among us; and yet
> Lives make and unmake themselves in her neighbourhood
> As nowhere else. There are many names I could name
> Who would have been remarkably otherwise
> Except for her divine non-interference.

This lightly-stressed yet unambiguous incarnation of God's respect for man's integrity, the divine letting-be, while holding grace in reserve for any human demand, brings the Countess into the company of the Duke in Shakespeare's *Measure for Measure*, that other providential figure who moves unobtrusively yet shapingly among his people. So secure is Fry's technique in this play that the scriptural references are made with the unstressed nonchalance of friendly conversation: Colonel

Janik, searching for the deserter Gettner, shows in one remark war's inversion of all values, even that of the Shepherd, with its Scriptural overtones:

> I have two thousand men
> Standing in the snow, their lives my trust.
> Peace may go in search of the one soul
> But we are not at peace.

Or the Countess, herself exiled to a stable from her cultivated home by the incursion of the 1848 war, with a gracious, un-emphatic irony recalls another stable:

> You put me under pain of enmity
> And have driven me out of my possessions,
> And yet this exile, though it is
> No more than a stable yard from home,
> Unites me with you, and with your soldiers.

But the core of the work is not the easy tact with which the Christian tradition is called into witty play; its core is the neces-sity for compassion, for the recognition of the particular in-tegrity of each human person, whether apparently good or apparently bad. It is proper that the Countess should make the central statement. Her long speech in Act I moves with co-herence, if with a deliberate renunciation of logic, through an implied argument with Janik. She begins with quiet reason-ableness:

> I am ready
> To be persuaded to your opinion
> By any truth which in God's world
> You can put before me . . .

She admits the necessity of changes in the society and the nations about them:

> I shall never make
> Myself, or my friends, my way of life
> Or private contentment, or any
> Preference of my nature, an obstacle
> To the needs of a more true and living world
> Than so far I have understood . . .

But the crux of the argument turns upon Janik, demanding that he apply the same standard to individual relationships that he expects in the conduct of States:

> To you Austria is a tyranny.
> Then, to the number of those men who die,
> And far beyond that number infinitely,
> Surely you will show
> One man over another has no kingdom.

Fry makes no pedantic references to a "just war" and its theological safeguards, but when war has broken her peace, the Countess touches allusively the courteous equivalent of this catholic doctrine:

> JANIK   You make
> Light of the ways of war, Countess.
>
> COUNTESS   I take them
> Seriously. And therefore I suppose them
> Reasonable, sensible, and civilized.

The springs of her compassionate integrity reveal themselves in one dramatic moment. Gettner, fugitive and demoralized, pleads that the company should not betray him.

> GETTNER   Have a respect for my life,
> For the sake of your sleep to come, don't betray me.
> Go to your imaginations, gentlemen:
> Think of death by shooting.
>
> BELMANN
> I should more likely weep for stags or partridges.
>
> COUNTESS
> Do, then. Weep for what you can.

The single phrase, "weep for what you can" holds the emotional pressure of so much of Fry's mature writing; he does not stay to argue the nature of relationships—it suffices that compassion seize any occasion for the practice of its grace.

This characteristic compassion operates within a strongly marked sense of time, of the process of history. There is no pedantry in the re-creation of the past but the past is always present: *The Lady* in "1400 either more or less or exactly", *The Dark is Light Enough* in the 1848 revolution, though its dilemmas are as old as our own and as contemporary as those of Pilate or Judas. An even greater assurance is found in *Curtmantle*. The search for law is timeless but if we compare Fry's handling of the theme with either Eliot's or Anouilh's we find the greater security in Fry's sense of historical fact—for Eliot was essentially concerned with the timeless matter of martyrdom, while Anouilh ignored the tensions of law for those of a relationship which could be set in any age. Even in the tact with which Fry seizes upon the complexity of Henry as the clue to the dramatic texture of the age, he is driven back by his probing of the historical material to a remarkable summary assessment of the king in the preface to the play:

> He was simple and royal, . . . direct and paradoxical, compassionate and hard, a man of intellect, a man of action, God-fearing, superstitious, blasphemous, far-seeing, short-sighted, affectionate, lustful, patient, volcanic, humble, overriding. It is difficult to think of any facet of man which at some time he didn't demonstrate, except chastity and sloth.

No other writer then has made such a comprehensive contribution to contemporary "religious drama" but no writer so elusively defies categorizing. In personal belief a committed Christian, Christopher Fry has not hesitated to employ drama, when the commission has come his way, in a clearly expository way, in *A Boy with a Cart, The Firstborn*, or *A Sleep of Prisoners*; but his characteristic playwright's manner is undogmatic, exploratory, and the play has been his instrument for exploration. The wit, the punning gaiety—which has sometimes looked so wilful as almost to seem irresponsible—has in fact been part of the equipment of a mind which never evades an awkward intellectual issue, sees certain dilemmas—such as the conflict of law and compassion—as pervasive but intolerable, and uses his craft to put forward solutions with a courteous and witty tact.

11

Contemporary Trends

This is an age rich in important drama and in imaginative experiment in theatre and in dramatic forms. It is moreover an age in which the theatre has been found once more to be an important form for the exploration of ideas and credal positions. It is therefore a matter of very nice critical discrimination on our part to determine, from the central point of view of this book, which are the more significant areas of dramatic writing, those which arise specifically from a position of religious assent, or those which explore on the frontiers of belief. We may put this question at its sharpest by questioning the relative interest —from a specifically and narrowly religious point of view and without passing judgements of literary value—of those plays which were produced immediately before the war at the Mercury Theatre (plays by Charles Williams, Ronald Duncan, Norman Nicholson, Anne Ridler) and the plays of Brecht, Pinter, or Samuel Beckett. This choice in fact begs two questions which ought to be cleared out of the way: on the one side some of these dramatists, notably Ronald Duncan, gave only a very qualified assent to the religious position which governed the thinking of most of them; on the other side, it is profoundly important not to blur distinctions by claiming a kind of crypto-Christianity for writers like Beckett on the very ambiguous ground that much of their imagery and some of their perhaps subconscious argument derives from traditional Christian sources. If we are to be faced with a valuable distinction which will be valid in any future consideration of the function and value of "religious drama", we must clarify and sharpen rather than blur distinctions. Thus the question worth putting at this moment is the relative importance in Christian thinking and Christian apologetic of works which are committed and expository, like Charles Williams' brief and brilliant *Seed of Adam* or *House by the Stable*, or those which explore the human condition without credal assumptions of any kind, works of the order of *The Caretaker*, *Camino Real*, or *Who's Afraid of Virginia Woolf?* To do justice to what must seem—indeed probably is—a loaded question, we should look a little more closely at what for convenience I have called the Mercury plays. It would in fact be more useful to associate together the aims of the sponsors of the Mercury Theatre plays, the work in general of the Religious Drama Society, and the intentions of the festivals like those of Canterbury and Chichester, together with the revivals of the medieval cycles at York, Coventry, and Chester.

The aim which they all have in common is that which motivated the medieval Church and the guilds in particular: to animate the creeds, to express in visible, in dramatic terms, the facts and values of the accepted body of scripture and belief. This is a seemly aim. Worship and meditation should engage a considerable range of man's faculties and participation in imaginative action enables this engagement to be fulfilled in peculiarly satisfying ways. But the assumption here is that our age presents conditions of common assumptions in belief and worship analogous with those of earlier ages; in fact we know that the extraordinary vitality of contemporary religious art springs from quite contrary conditions, not common assumptions but the mental and spiritual strains and tensions which arise from "arguing out" the matter of the faith in the presence of sceptical unbelief, and in symbols and media which are not the private preserve of Christian artists.

This will be seen very clearly by considering the popular esteem of so much of the work which has gone into Coventry Cathedral. Much of it is derived from strictly traditional iconography, and this element comes to its splendid conclusion in Graham Sutherland's tapestry, every moment of which is a personal interpretation of the most central of our iconographical traditions. But one other work in particular, the very large window designed by John Piper for the baptistry, owes little or nothing to this tradition save the stained-glass medium itself with its emotional overtones and certain very broad symbolic associations of colour. Yet this window the aesthetic sources of which are wholly in the range of modern abstract art, is probably the work which has aroused the greatest, most universal admiration in the whole cathedral. Indeed, the potent names in the revival of religious art in our day, Rouault, Matisse, Moore, Piper, Sutherland, and, in certain recent developments, Barbara Hepworth, demonstrate the two wholly disparate lines along which fruitful development can apparently go—by the extension of a vital tradition into our own day or, on the contrary, by adapting to the old context the newer modes and techniques which in most hands owe nothing to religious concepts, and indeed, in their abstraction deny the conceptual altogether.

A similar distinction has been implicit throughout the argument of this book. On the one hand dramatic forms have been used vigorously to expound intellectual positions which are common ground for the artist and his audience. At other ages, notably in Shakespeare's and our own, the universality of traditional beliefs is questioned; speculation has its greatest imaginative value not at the centre but at the periphery of belief, a fact of most uncomfortable implications to the conservative mind of the Church.

This very simple distinction should assist in clarifying the rather ambiguous attitude of the Church towards the function

of art, and hence in clarifying its patronage. The function of the
Christian play, poem, or picture within the Church is tolerably
clear; by the clarity, the sensitive integrity of its form and content, it expresses the faith at its richest and most complex. This
is the "function" which gives its classical quality as religious
art to the *Divine Comedy*, to *Secunda Pastorum*, to the *Last Judg-
ment*. But what is the Christian critic to say to *King Lear*, to
Byron's *Cain*, to *Mother Courage*, to *Godot*? Can any appeal to
expressive function, to the imaginative bodying out of the
creed, express their vital importance to Christian thinking?
Yet these works have manifestly an importance to serious religious thinking far beyond their less disturbing fellows in the
faith. Charles Williams' *House of the Octopus*, Norman Nicholson's *Old Man of the Mountains*, Ronald Duncan's *This Way to the
Tomb* all performed an important function in clarifying some
of the implications of the faith to the faithful or at least to
those who were predisposed to ask the traditional questions;
so did *Murder in the Cathedral* at a profounder level, this play
too deriving some of its original impetus from its being commissioned by the Canterbury Festival. But the Church is not an
enclosed society; the maturity of its thinking in any age depends upon the validity and comprehensiveness of its response to movements, social, intellectual, artistic, which appear
to deny its fundamental affirmations. I am interested in a
bishop's response to Claudel or Eliot; I am far more interested
in his response to Beckett, Albee, or Genet—or indeed whether
he has any response at all. For it is the latter who constitute the
periphery, the context of the faith in our day; this is the area,
serious, agonized in its exploration, within which the faith
must be seen to be relevant, if it is not to be seen as a cosy ex-
change of irrefutable platitudes between the like-minded. For
myself, I foresee a far less useful function for the traditional
form of religious drama in the immediate future. It is clear that
liturgical experiment along the lines of the earliest tropes could

greatly enhance the imaginative quality of public worship, and there is certainly room for the major artists, of the order of Benjamin Britten, to create for the Church such quasi-dramatic works as his *War Requiem*. But the critical endeavour of the Church is needed, not in fostering amateur expression of the accepted truths of the faith but in exploring the implications of the great non-Christian works which handle the massive spiritual dilemmas. Here the significant names will all be outside the central tradition we have hitherto examined; the critical discipline will consist not in verifying degrees of assent, in tracing the lines of significant symbol, but in distinguishing the intensities of dissent, in charting the techniques within which fruitful experiment is being undertaken.

To express this more particularly: it should have been clear from the last two chapters that the work of T. S. Eliot and Christopher Fry, in stating in dramatic terms for the secular theatre of Shaftesbury Avenue and Broadway the complexities of belief, has a permanent value. At the same time it is clear that the bases of their faith are too secure, too confident for universal acceptance, that the disorientated mind cannot begin with their assumptions. The Christian will realize that *Family Reunion* and *Curtmantle* raise problems, investigate dilemmas, to which the creeds of the Church give no clear-cut immediate answers; but behind the dilemmas stand the broad securities and affirmations of the sacraments and of natural law theology. This is not common territory for the theatre-goer. For him the dilemmas of Brecht, Albee, or Genet will be more radical, more consonant with his condition.

This is seen most clearly in the area of tragic drama. The condition of Job, Oedipus, and Lear was, at its point of greatest dereliction, still comprehensible, part of a cosmic pattern; it was neither meaningless nor "absurd" in the modern sense of the word. But tragedy has to-day taken on a new dimension. It is precisely the quality of absurd incomprehension that makes it most difficult to accept as in any sense cathartic or even "significant". With the decay of a theology of suffering and the more widespread awareness of hunger, disease, and mass destruction, the temper in which the relation of sainthood and martyrdom can be argued out in the moderation of verse in *Murder in the Cathedral*, has become almost wholly irrelevant. Nathan Scott recently (January 1963) argued out this background in *The Anglican Theological Review* in an essay, "The Tragic Vision and the Christian Faith":

> The world of tragic experience, in other words, is a world presided over by clashing antinomies, by tensions and antagonisms that are ontological as well as moral: its people live under the dominance of potencies which are veiled and therefore vaguely menacing. It is a world of mystery and insecurity, of anxiety and dread, for the executive powers to which man owes his loyalty are powers that are themselves involved in opposition to one another. So the human protagonist finds himself to be fundamentally uncertain as to the relation in which he stands to the transcendently real: the spheres of man's self-experience and of ultimate reality are sundered, and the commerce between them moves obscurely and unpredictably, in a way that eludes any conceptual chart.

In these circumstances, where Eliot, Fry, Charles Williams, or even Ronald Duncan may appear to assume theological standpoints which the modern theatregoer is reluctant to accept, Genet or Albee are strictly relevant to their condition. The nightmare world of Kafka, the tragic probings of Camus, even the total amorality of Genet are immediately pertinent—and the Christian critic would be far more advised to explore the implications of their impact on the contemporary consciousness than the better-charted areas of classical theology and its dramatic expression.

At this point the drama of Bertolt Brecht assumes outstanding significance. The historical perspective of *Mother Courage*, never insistent but never overlooked, maintains a traditional pattern of intellectual reference even when Brecht's thinking is at its most ironic and subversive. Of the younger generation of English writers Harold Pinter preserves this precarious balance best. In all his work, if most notably in *The Caretaker*, he has achieved the very difficult feat of making inarticulacy articulate, of giving shapely dramatic expression to the un-dramatic, unformed fumblings of speech. But the plays themselves have a tightly-knit traditional structure, a framework within which the tragic gropings are distanced and made com-prehensible. Samuel Beckett maintains a similar equilibrium in the two-act symmetry of *Waiting for Godot*, with its teasing, half-formulated symbolisms. These are certainly the drama-tists most intellectually accessible to the contemporary public as the theatre finds its way into a formulation of our spiritual dilemmas.

From the point of view of this essay two dramatists have posed awkward problems in single plays, Robert Bolt in *A Man for all Seasons* and John Osborne in *Luther*, problems which are simply intensified by the comparison which is almost inevit-able with Brecht's *Galileo*. Eliot began his exploration of Becket, as did Fry his Henry II, from common presuppositions, an acceptance of intellectual and spiritual affinities between the dramatist and his subject which made an historical sympathy possible. Osborne's Luther is without any such sympathetic in-sight (ironically enough Tetzel is a far better realized figure) while even Robert Bolt, who cannot be accused of exploiting More for theatrical purposes, yet wrests him into the expres-sion of twentieth-century dilemmas, extruding the significant area of intellectual conflict which make him significantly the scholar-saint and equivocal statesman of the sixteenth century. More especially in Osborne, but to a degree in Bolt, the secular instrument which the theatre has become, appears ill-suited to dissect essentially spiritual dilemmas. It is yet another irony of twentieth-century drama that the Marxist Bertolt Brecht reaches a far more delicate insight into the standpoint of the Church than many dramatists achieve in the more traditional West.

This book approaches only a few of the critical issues raised by the term "Religious Drama". There are major figures who demand assessment from this standpoint: Tennessee Williams, whose *Camino Real* approaches as near religious allegory as any modern American play; Arthur Miller whose *Crucible* translates religious intolerance into assimilable if painfully crude modern terms; and the whole range of the "theatre of the absurd" confronts our more comfortable traditional values.

At the same time the newer instruments of expression in radio, cinema, and ballet set their own problems. Macneice's *The Dark Tower* in sound radio, a number of television experiments, notably Lawrence Waddy's *Job*, have hitherto been given the aloof condescension too often accorded to the "mass media". Even the "epic" religious film requires serious evaluation, with much of its power still unrealized.

And still the classics confront us, as we attempt our contemporary reappraisal. If we are prepared to concede to art the rôle of clarification and imaginative exploration, as man is teased by the ambiguities and ironies of his condition, then *Antigone*, the *Shepherds' Play*, *Macbeth* remain among the potent forms of theological insight; this is a tradition which the theatre still maintains in our own day.

A Short Book-List

This subject is of such vast proportions that it seems impossible even to embark on a reading list. It is of course always better to read original texts than literary criticism, but the following books are suggested as helpful in those periods that need some background scholarship to give them their full meaning.

When Sophocles' *Antigone* has been studied, his other plays should be explored, together with selections from Aeschylus, and from Euripides, followed by one or two critical works, and in particular:

H. D. F. Kitto. *Form and Meaning in Drama*. New York: Barnes and Noble, 1957.

This is of general importance on religious drama; Kitto should also be read in two related critical works:

Greek Tragedy. New York: Doubleday Anchor Books, 1954.
Sophocles, Dramatist and Philosopher. New York: Oxford University Press, 1958.

On the more general theory of Greek tragedy:

John Jones. *On Aristotle and Greek Tragedy*. New York: Oxford University Press, 1962.

Medieval religious drama should be read widely; fundamental critical works to be consulted are:

Karl Young. *Drama of the Medieval Church*, 2 vols. New York: Oxford University Press, 1933.
Hardin Craig. *English Religious Drama of the Middle Ages*. New York: Oxford University Press, 1955.

And for the general literary background:

G. R. Owst. *Literature and Pulpit in Medieval England,* 2nd rev. ed. New York: Barnes and Noble, 1961.

E. K. Chambers. *English Literature at the Close of the Middle Ages.* New York: Oxford University Press, 1945.

Critical controversy over the theological background to Elizabethan and Jacobean drama has intensified during the past year or so, and there is a dissident book by Roland Mushat Frye, *Shakespeare and Christian Doctrine* (Princeton: Princeton University Press, 1963) which should be read not for its criticism but for its references and bibliography. Still by far the best introduction to this aspect of Shakespearean drama is:

G. Wilson Knight. *The Wheel of Fire.* New York: Meridian Books (first published in 1930).

The ablest brief introduction to *Samson Agonistes* is the handbook:

J. B. Broadbent. *Milton: Comus and Samson Agonistes.* Great Neck, N.Y.: Barron's Educational Series, Inc., 1961 (see particularly its brief book-list).

Little of real value has been written on religious drama in the Romantic and Victorian period but Wilson Knight is always stimulating on Byron.

Modern religious drama from Eliot to our immediate contemporaries has been prolific. The best introduction to Eliot's plays remains:

David Jones. *The Plays of T. S. Eliot.* Toronto: University of Toronto Press, 1960.

And for the American scene (with parallel studies in European literature) see in particular:

Finley Eversole (ed.). *Christian Faith and the Contemporary Arts.* Nashville: Abingdon Press, 1962.

Nathan Scott (ed.). *The Climate of Faith in Modern Literature.* New York: Seabury Press, 1964.

Type, 10 on 12 Bembo
Display, Bembo
Paper, Antique 'R'

Date Due